Managing by Priority

Managing by Priority

Thinking Strategically, Acting Effectively

Giorgio Merli

JOHN WILEY & SONS

Chichester · New York · Brisbane · Toronto · Singapore

Original Italian edition published under the title of
Il Manager Imprenditore (Management by Priority,
Breakthrough, BPR: I nuovi metodi per gestire il migliora mento aziendale)
Copyright © 1995 Il Sole 24 Pirola Spa

English language edition
copyright © 1996 by John Wiley & Sons Ltd,
      Baffins Lane, Chichester,
      West Sussex PO19 1UD, England

      National   01243 779777
      International (+44) 1243 779777
      e-mail (for orders and customer service enquiries): cs-books@wiley.co.uk
      Visit our Home Page on http://www. wiley.co.uk
            or http://www.wiley.com

Other Wiley Editorial Offices

John Wiley & Sons, Inc., 605 Third Avenue,
New York, NY 10158-0012, USA

Jacaranda Wiley Ltd, 33 Park Road, Milton,
Queensland 4064, Australia

John Wiley & Sons (Canada) Ltd, 22 Worcester Road,
Rexdale, Ontario M9W 1L1, Canada

John Wiley & Sons (Asia) Pte Ltd, 2 Clementi Loop #02-01,
Jin Xing Distripark, Singapore 129809

Library of Congress Cataloging-in-Publication Data
Merli, Giorgio.
    (Manager imprenditore. English)
    Managing by priority: thinking strategically, acting effectively / Giorgio Merli
      p. cm.
    Includes bibliograpical references and index.
      ISBN 0-471-96656-8 (cloth)
      1. Strategic planning: I. Title
    HD30.28.M45813   1996
    658.4'012—dc20   96–28873
                                                  CIP
British Library Cataloguing in Publication Data

A catalogue record for this book is available from the British Library

ISBN 0 471 96656 8

Typeset in 11/13pt Palatino from the author's disks by Saxon Graphics Limited, Derby
Printed and bound in Great Britain by Bookcraft (Bath) Ltd, Midsomer Norton, Somerset.
This book is printed on acid-free paper responsibly manufactured from sustainable forestation,
for which at least two trees are planted for each one used for paper production.

To my son Gabriele

Contents

Preface and Acknowledgements

When we examine the world's most successful companies we are left in no doubt of the following considerations:

- Strategic planning has given way to strategic thinking
- The strategy of continuous improvement (Kaizen) has been complemented by the need for Breakthroughs
- Management by Objectives has led the way to Management by Policies and Management by Breakthroughs
- Numerical targets have ceased to be the only priority. Nowadays managers also focus on "how" to achieve these targets so as to ensure maximum operative and strategic consistency (through policies)
- Management is no longer based on the control of all the operational activities; priorities are now key and a special management system is utilized to achieve them
- Managers have turned their focus upstream and are scrutinizing the "levers" which cause results, instead of applying the ex post approach, which starts when something has already happened. Thus we learn the Japanese lesson: managing by causes rather than by results
- Management by function has been superseded by management by business process
- Management control is now looking to Activity Based Management, and focusing their attention on performance drivers

- Budgeting by cost centres as well as analytical management control are now used just to set up projection forecasting data and to check the trend of the operational indicators.

We could summarize all these considerations by stating that there is trend away from management focused on "optimization" at all costs, to a more selective, "entrepreneurial" approach. Nowadays companies are making a deliberate effort to devise management systems that reproduce the mental processes of entrepreneurs running small businesses. This consists of:

- Setting priorities
- Concentrating on these and delegating everything else
- Deciding the best ways to carry out the priorities with operational and strategic consistency
- Motivating the personnel to be involved
- Achieving significant results – fast

In this book I will provide an interpretation of the management systems being used in the most successful companies, as well as the trends that are currently emerging. In addition I will offer a reference model for entrepreneurial business management.

As well as being a guide to the entire process of the entrepreneurial rationale, this book places particular stress on some examples of best practice and contains advice on how to manage effectively. I will attempt to create a reference model which is both universally applicable and relatively simple. The aim is very specific: to provide a comprehensive system to those who wish to run their companies as "entrepreneurs".

I am talking about an approach that combines the entrepreneurial rationale with the management processes. It guarantees that control processes do not take precedence over operational management, and entrepreneurial thinking is not frustrated by an absence of effective procedures and support systems.

The book is addressed to two types of reader:

1 Owners and senior managers of medium-sized companies who wish to implement a more systematic approach to their management system without, however, having to renounce their creative and spontaneous skills

2 CEOs and senior managers working in large organizations, who wish to adopt a more entrepreneurial style of management

The contents of this book are based on three sources of know-how:

1 Examples of "best practice" as employed by leading companies worldwide
2 My own personal experience acquired through my consultancy work
3 The latest trends emerging from, and being implemented in, some of the most innovative-minded businesses throughout the world.

I have used the following sources of information:

1. *Best practice leader companies/success stories.* I have extensively referred to the management systems used by Rank Xerox (winner of Total Quality awards both in the USA and in Europe), Hewlett Packard (one of the first companies to have successfully transposed Japanese management systems for use in a non-Japanese environment), Toyota (the undisputed world leader in innovative organizational and management systems), Sony (the most "Western" of the Japanese companies), Whirlpool (world leader in the white appliances field), Michelin (an example of "excellence" in production quality and efficiency), SGS-Thomson (the only European microprocessor manufacturer that can compete on equal terms with American and Japanese producers), Allied Signal (widely adopting these systems since 1995), as well as a number of successful small and medium-sized European companies.
2. *First-hand experience gained with Galgano & Associates.* I have concentrated on the most successful examples of the consultancy work of Galgano & Associates, highlighting the recipes that enabled us to achieve the best results. From a sample of

over three hundred cases, I have selected about forty success stories.(*)

3. *Emerging strategic, organizational and management methods.* These can be summarized as the more entrepreneurial aspects of various management factors. By entrepreneurial I mean that formality is reduced to a minimum, only the elements considered most important are used, operational tools are stressed. Here are some of the factors:

- Strategic approaches: strategic thinking, planning by priority, specific innovative aspects of business processes (such as Lean Production, Comakership, Concurrent Engineering and Demand Driven Logistics)
- Organizational approaches: Business Process Re-engineering, Value Analysis and Zero Base Planning;
- Management approaches: Management by Policy/Hoshin Kanri, Effective Management, the SEDAC system and Management by Processes

Acknowledgements

There are a number of other important sources of information which, while being less technical and less objectively quantifiable, are nonetheless extremely important. They are:

- Executives in companies with which I have been involved who provided experience and have agreed to my quoting their cases

---

* I would like to quote the following references (with sector and one year achievements): Motorcycles: technical assistance costs –20%; quality +80%; time to market –50%; Bank: deposits 50% above industry average; Wall-mounted boilers: quality +80%; WIP –60%; Lead Times –50%; Distribution pharmaceuticals: market share +2.5%; stocks –20%; Synthetic fibres: cash flow +50%; Telecommunications: costs –15%; quality +50%; Lead Times –30%; Cars: stocks –50%; quality +80%; Local government offices: productivity +16%; Car spares: Lead Times and stocks –60%; Shipbuilding: management of turnaround breakthrough in bottom line; Car components: quality +80%; Tyres: productivity +15%p.a.; Tyres: fixed industrial costs –30%; Micro chips: Lead Times –50%; quality +90%; Factory-packaged foodstuffs: Machinery productivity +11%; Electrodes: productivity +35%; quality +90%; Hospital: pharmaceutical costs +50%; materials costs –40%.

- My colleagues at Galgano & Associates together with whom I have gained the knowledge and expertise on which this book is based
- Ryuji Fukuda, the best mentor one could ever have, who taught me about the practical approaches to improving performance

I also want to thank Ruth Hunt Martinez, who managed the translation of this book from the Italian edition and Bob Millar for reviewing it. Particular acknowledgements must go to Carlalberto Da Pozzo, Marco Biroli, Andrea Di Lenna and Barbara Bellotta for their contributions.

1
Requisites for Success

In talking about success or diagnosing its causes I like to refer to three basic principles: the "Relativity" Principle; the "Priority" Principle and the "Effectiveness" Principle.

THE "RELATIVITY" PRINCIPLE

"Success is by definition a relative thing. It is always determined by situations where there is an advantage over the competition." Such a definition must clearly include both cases in which a company generates higher profits than its competitors and cases in which, in times of recession, it loses less. The general market situation on its own can only indicate average values, not the relative facts. This is not such a negligible thing, however, because it determines the "minimum" performance level necessary to participate in a business field in a given period (for example, price/cost ratio, quality levels, delivery times, innovational content of products services). It also conditions the "absolute value" of the economic result (determining in practice the average profitability level of the sector over the period) and it determines the market performance improvement trend, as a sectorial average (prices, quality, delivery times). This trend is the "dynamic" reference zero (the trend necessary to maintain the same level of relative competitivity).

THE "PRIORITY" PRINCIPLE

It is a fact that in highly competitive situations "the competitive advantage may be achieved and maintained only if the right improvement priorities (objectives and/or levers) are chosen". The following quotation, attributed to the chairperson of a famous multinational company in the computer sector, is significant: "I'm tired of seeing presentations demonstrating that fantastic improvements have been made in operative performance when the company's bottom line is worsening all the time! If I accept that your data are exact, I must conclude that either what you have improved is only a small part of the activities of your unit or you have used the wrong lever to get the results the company really needs!"

THE "EFFECTIVENESS" PRINCIPLE

"Success is greatly conditioned by the capacity to achieve Breakthroughs on priority performances." In fact success is almost always reached by improving a key performance or by making a radical change.

Both the Priority Principle and the Effectiveness Principle can also be defined as "entrepreneurial" principles. In fact what does a successful entrepreneur do? He or she concentrates on a small number of priorities, where he or she tries to achieve high level results and delegates other objectives.

Keeping in mind the above three principles, most success situations can be explained by the following logics:

- The company possesses a competitive advantage
- This is due to successful actions taken in the past
- These actions were successful because they were carried out on the key factors of the company's business,
- The extent of the results obtained on these factors was certainly considerable

It may be concluded that success requires the capacity to identify the right priorities and the ability to know how to obtain important results on them. Having said this, it is easy to understand the comment by the general manager of an office automation firm, who said: "To be sure of success it's not enough to find the right strategies, choose the right objectives, prepare ambitious plans. If these things don't produce real Breakthroughs in the firm's operations we'll simply find ourselves with a fine book of dreams in our hands."

It must be realized, however, that learning to work by priorities and obtaining results are not just a question of method. It means learning quite a different approach from that normally adopted. In fact, concentrating on only a few priorities means taking a fair degree of risk. Besides this, achieving top-level results presupposes considerable management effectiveness. Risk and management effectiveness are synonyms of entrepreneurial management.

This type of management has three basic stages:

1 Identifying the priorities and the relative objectives
2 Identifying the actions necessary to pursue them
3 Managing with operative effectiveness

These stages will be described in the following chapters. The keyword used in the description of the proposed approach is "Breakthrough". It is the word that defines the special character of entrepreneurial management in that it includes both the concept of priorities and that of radical improvement.

2
The Breakthrough Approach

To apply the Breakthrough approach in practice, we must take into consideration the types of action necessary to obtain the required results. Clearly a reorganization, for example, will be managed very differently from an operational intervention on activities already in course. So it may be useful to describe this approach through its possible practical and operative dimensions, which can be identified as follows (Figure 2.1):

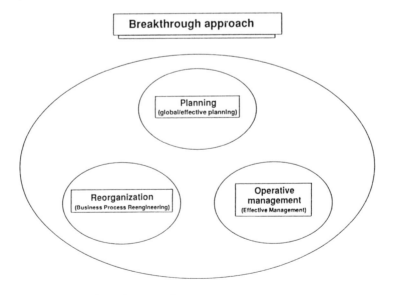

Figure 2.1   *Breakthrough approach.*

- Choosing the priorities and planning the actions
- Carrying out the reorganizational steps
- Carrying out the operational steps

These are specific methods, to be adopted in periods of special management. However, as will be seen later, they can also be profitably transformed into a systematic management method.

PLANNING

During a period of "special management", planning simply means choosing the priorities on which to intervene to achieve the desired Breakthrough results. When the company is in "normal running conditions" it will systematically plan by priorities. The elements to be planned will be the usual ones in both cases (Figure 2.2), such as changes in strategies for competitive advantage, product, market, make or buy, value chain, and so on.

The approach has a precise output, however: the Breakthrough plan. These new planning methods in special management periods are illustrated in Chapter 3 of the book. The normal running methods (Planning by Vision and by Policy) are dealt with elsewhere.*

REORGANIZING

This involves large-scale action on company organization (Figure 2.3). Reorganizing objectives generally aim at improving either output performance (e.g. time to market, production time, delivery time, product/service quality, market response capacity, and so on) or structure costs.

The method considered most effective today is the "by business processes" approach. This means obtaining the required results by taking specific action on the series of sequential, value-added activities (the process) that determine the performance in question. This approach is preferred today also in structure cost reduction because it enables correct value analyses to be made of

---

* G. Merli, *Breakthrough Management*, John Wiley & Sons, Chichester 1995 and – *EuroChallenge, IFS Ltd.*, Bedford 1993

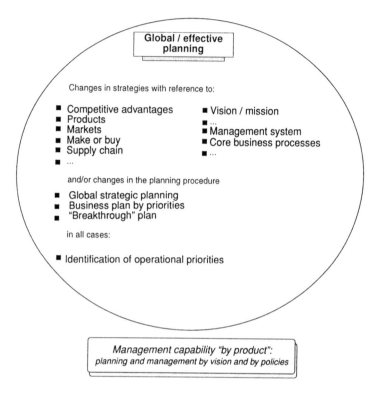

Figure 2.2   *Planning.*

the activities, thus avoiding unbalanced or indiscriminate intervention on all the company's sectors. Designing, delivering and marketing, are all examples of processes.

Tackling reorganizing plans through the business process rationale, with the objective of achieving radical improvements, means adopting the Business Process Reengineering (BPR) approach. This method is very "fashionable" in the business world today, but it is also full of substance, as we shall see.

BPR action can be directed towards three basic types of Breakthrough objective:

- Radical reduction in structure costs
- Rapid alignment with best competitor performance
- Obtaining a undisputable competitive advantage

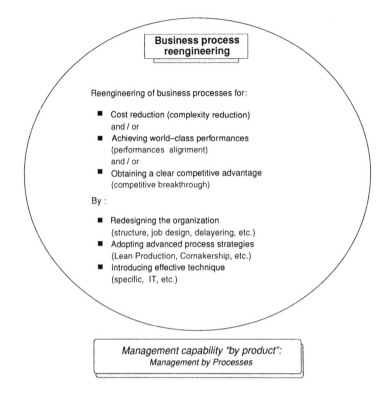

Business process reengineering

Reengineering of business processes for:

- Cost reduction (complexity reduction) and / or
- Achieving world–class performances (performances alignment) and / or
- Obtaining a clear competitive advantage (competitive breakthrough)

By :

- Redesigning the organization (structure, job design, delayering, etc.)
- Adopting advanced process strategies (Lean Production, Comakership, etc.)
- Introducing effective technique (specific, IT, etc.)

Management capability "by product":
Management by Processes

Figure 2.3   *Reorganization.*

The actions necessary can be divided into the following three types:

1 Structural and organizational revision at company level (either general or just for the priority processes)
2 Adoption of specific strategic process approaches (for example Lean Production, Comakership, Concurrent Engineering)
3 Adoption of specific methods and procedures (including changes in data processing systems)

The BPR approach will be illustrated in Chapter 4 while in Chapter 7 I will deal with the Management by Product of BPR, that is, Management by Processes (a systematic operational procedure to improve company's business processes continuously).

OPERATIONAL ACTIONS

Most Breakthrough objectives do not require changes in the structure but "simply" a radical improvement in operational performance, given the same organization chart and business procedures (Figure 2.4). In this case a special type of management process must be activated, aimed at obtaining the required results quickly. The short time span and the priorities policy mean that the normal mechanisms of budgeting, management control and the classical Management by Objectives cannot be

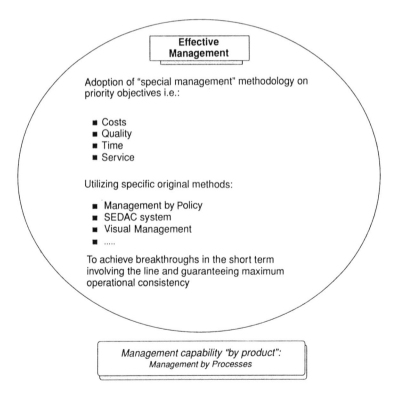

Effective Management

Adoption of "special management" methodology on priority objectives i.e.:

- Costs
- Quality
- Time
- Service

Utilizing specific original methods:

- Management by Policy
- SEDAC system
- Visual Management
- .....

To achieve breakthroughs in the short term involving the line and guaranteeing maximum operational consistency

Management capability "by product":
Management by Processes

Figure 2.4   *Operative management.*

used. Different methods are required, in particular a more effective management system.

The objectives referred to in this case normally concern such factors as quality, costs, times, services or results to achieve in areas like sales, the working capital, cash flow, and so on. The method suggested, called Effective Management, applies diverse instruments, some well known, others less. They range from Policy Deployment to the SEDAC system and Visual Management. This form of special management can also be transformed into a systematic management mechanism defined as Management by Policy. Effective Management will be illustrated in Chapter 5 and Management by Policy in Chapter 7.

THE BREAKTHROUGH APPROACH REQUISITES

To be successful a Breakthrough approach must guarantee effectiveness over the short term and also coherence over the medium to long term. Clearly it must be capable of activating a high level of company resource mobilization on the priorities concerned. It will be all the more successful if it activates learning organization capabilities, that is, if it is able to disseminate at each management cycle (3, 6 or 12 months) greater operative capacity.

Encouraged by the success of numerous experiences in the field, the approach I illustrate in this book will aim at fulfilling all these requirements.

3
Planning Objectives and Actions

THE APPROACH

Planning means choosing. In a Breakthrough approach it means choosing the priorities on which to act; that is, the levers most suitable for achieving the required results. As mentioned in the preceding chapter, I will illustrate the methods for preparing a plan of Breakthroughs – a plan to achieve important results over the short and medium term.

The planned (chosen) actions must have the following characteristics:

- Operational effectiveness (important results and ease in obtaining them)
- Action coherence/synergy (to avoid waste and apply the effort involved in the best way)
- Guaranteed contribution to competitiveness in the medium to long term

PLANNING "HORIZONS"

It may be worthwhile first to recall some of the business planning concepts concerning the problem of the coherence between actions and the contribution to competitiveness in the medium term. A first consideration, as stated previously, is that a successful plan guarantees the company an increased cash flow in the short term but also competitiveness over the medium to long term.*

In fact a company which takes out too much in the short term, prejudicing its own future is a loser, as is one which ignores short-term results while pursuing medium and long-term success (in the meantime, it closes down!). A high level of coherence and synergy between actions over a period of time is therefore necessary. As we well know, however, the planning and management scenario can be disturbed by a further ingredient, emergencies, which by definition are unplannable. The effective approach reconciles the capacity to manage emergencies with the need to meet the financial objectives of the future. For this we need what we may call an "entrepreneurial" approach capable of identifying those priorities and policies which can ensure operating coherence over time.

With reference to time, it consists of the ability to pursue effectively objectives with three different horizons (short, medium and long term) and at the same time manage emergency situations. This means the simultaneous management of actions which will have their impact at different points in time (Figure 3.1).

The basic needs to manage effectively and coherently are:

- Emergencies
- The priority objectives derived from the annual business plan (defined as short-term objectives)
- The medium-term priority objectives (normally derived from the strategic plan or a strategic "vision")
- The future of the business (whose objectives are not derived from any strategic plan, but from entrepreneurial "creeds")

This last requirement recalls the Japanese entrepreneurs, who claim that they plan their business over 10–11 year horizons. How do they do it? They certainly do not plan in numbers over 10 years! They plan their "creeds". Examples of these are flexibility, customer satisfaction, the cultivation of global managers

---

*See G. Merli, *Breakthrough Management*, John Wiley & Sons, Chichester 1995.

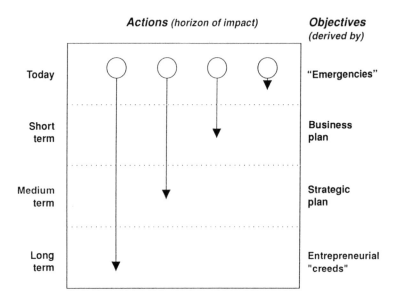

Figure 3.1 *Effective entrepreneurial approach.*

instead of specialists, etc. The fact that such policies will improve the financial results of the firm cannot be demonstrated mathematically, but the entrepreneur knows it, "he believes it".

Let us now look at a few examples which illustrate what I mean by emergencies, short-, medium- and long-term objectives (Figure 3.2). An emergency normally consists of a problem to be solved or opportunities to be seized. It is something which must be tackled or solved at top speed. Examples of emergencies are a factory stoppage, an invitation to tender or a complaint from an important customer. More generally it is something to be "caught on the wing" or to "take it or leave it", or, more often, a "big problem to solve". In these situations there is no scientific method to be applied. Here competitive advantage depends on the capacity for improvisation, for quicker reaction than the others (and in these cases the West excels).

Now let us look at some examples of short-term objectives. These are usually aimed at the improvement of operating performance, impacting on current-year financial results. For example, reduce costs by 10%, improve quality by 40%, increase

Examples of goals by "horizon"

Emergencies	Short term	Medium term	Long term
· Removal of problems · Seizing opportunities	· Improvement of operational performances	· Improvement of operational performance capabilities	· Improvement of strategic capabilities
Examples: - Quality problems - Production breakdown - Customer complaint - Important proposal - Customized product	Examples (indicators): - Costs - Sales - Process quality - Times - Volumes - Market share - Productivity ·- Stocks -	Examples (indicators): - Lead Times - Time to market - Process capability - Flexibility - Customer satisfaction - Technological improvement	- Human resource capabilities - Technological Breakthroughs - Market strategies

Figure 3.2   *Example of goals by horizon.*

sales by 5%, reduce order-filling time by 50%, increase production volume by 20%, increase market share by 3%, increase productivity by 15%, reduce stocks by 30%.

These are common examples of annual objectives set by companies today. What then are medium-term objectives? They are those objectives which ensure that the business will still be competitive in two to three years time. What are they concerned with? Usually with improvements to the capabilities of the organization which will have an impact on its competitiveness; that is, improvements which will only be reflected in terms of financial results after a few years. The problem of identifying medium-term priorities lies in the difficulty of understanding where the business is potentially exposed to competition in a scenario projected two or three years hence, and in deciding which features of competitive advantage should be pursued in such a scenario. Among the objectives which aim at medium-term competitiveness, we often find time to market, that is new product development time. It is obvious that the reduction of this sort of time-scale will only have an impact on business results after a number of years. It will become evident only when the new product begins to generate higher revenues than competitors products, thanks to its level of "relative" innovation.

Another typical medium-term objective is the reduction of Manufacturing Lead Time. An example of this type of objective would be the capability to manufacture and deliver a product within two weeks from receipt of order, where previously it was manufactured against sales forecast (generating large stocks of finished products). However, even this type of advantage can only be exploited effectively in the market place after suitable marketing, probably not before the following year.

A further example of a medium-term objective is customer satisfaction. It is clear that satisfied customers today mean a guarantee of further order the next time round (the life cycle time depends on the type of product). By contrast, *pushing a customer* unduly is an example of a bad short-term objective: it ensures the best possible result for the current year, but probably a loss of market share in the following years. How many firms could tell the tale of how they took advantage of the customer to make the maximum out of him for a year, and then lost market share over the medium term!

Other examples of medium-term objectives are improvements in technology or in process capabilities, and improvements in quality of service.

So far as long-term objectives are concerned, the basic question to help identify them is "what will our company be like in five to ten years time?" The Japanese reply would be "it will be exactly what the firm's employees are able to do; it will be the result of their capabilities and nothing else". This implies that the process of developing new senior and middle managers and new workers becomes very important. We must concern ourselves today with preparing the right people who will know how to carry us forward in the future in the direction in which we wish to go. If we are thinking of a future where the firm must be more "flexible", we must be sure to develop a culture of flexibility, and not one of functional specializations.

If we want a business with a great capacity for sensing and understanding market needs, we must create the capacity to decode weak market signals. This capacity is linked with a certain type of person, but also with certain types of methodology and organization (for which we must start planning today). There may also be issues of technology, or a combination of technology and market. Once these factors have been identified, we must decide and plan how to pursue them.

Consider for a moment those firms which start by deciding on what they want to produce, then about the organization required, and finally about the people that they must find. This is a back-to-front process, more suited to milking a business in the short to medium term than to preparing it to be a long-term winner.

To be precise, the organizational and cultural shape which we want to create over the long term is today commonly termed "vision". The vision represents the image of the firm which we should "like" to create over the next five to 10 years. It represents what we consider to be the winner for the future and is usually expressed as guiding principles, policies, types of organization with reference to the operating capacities of the firm, such as maximum customer satisfaction, flexibility, learning organization, flat structure, Management by Processes, Management by Policy, Simultaneous Engineering, etc. The objectives and, in consequence, the actions to be taken to pursue this vision can then be defined as "long-term objectives". A large part of these objectives and actions depend on the development of the capabilities of people, so it is understandable that a five- to 10-year planning horizon (or "vision") is necessary in order to achieve them.

CHOOSING HORIZON-BASED ACTIONS

Returning to the classification of objectives into the three time scales of short, medium and long term, the practical planning viewpoint is that to ensure the success of a business we must be able to plan and implement simultaneous, effective actions which make their impact on all three horizons, using the right mix of effort. Indeed, since we cannot supervise hundreds of short-, medium- and long-term objectives, we must limit the number and choose only those that are most important. We must also decide how much effort and cash are right and opportune for us to invest in the short, medium and long term, in our own business and at a given moment in time. The answer is not a simple one, and it depends on one or two basic considerations. The problem of the mix (that is, how much resource/commitment/effort to dedicate to objectives over the three horizons) is indeed a critical part of the planning process. It has a major impact on the choice of the number of objectives and on their nature. Yet there is no scientific method for tackling such a problem. However, it is possible to give a few points of reference. In broad terms it could be said that a "normal" company, steaming ahead in calm waters should be fairly concerned with the short term, but particularly concerned with ensuring its success in two or three years time. It is on this horizon that the company should be concentrating. On the other hand, a company with major short-term problems or priorities (a situation I deal with in detail in this book) can certainly not afford to lower its guard on its current operating results. It is clear that for this type of firm the level of effort will be greater for the short term than for the other horizons. It would, however, be a mistake to conclude that this type of firm cannot afford the luxury of choosing any medium- to long-term priority objectives because it cannot dedicate resources to them.

In reality this firm should be even more "entrepreneurial" and aware than others. Since it can only dedicate limited resources to the medium to long term, it must have a very clear idea of what is most important. It must choose accurately, since it cannot commit itself to many objectives. One objective will be more than enough and will already be an effort to pursue. Thus, it must be the right one. It is therefore not true that a company with short-term difficulties should be managed by someone who is good only at rigorous short-term action. This firm needs two types of management capacity: high short-term effectiveness and also highly entrepreneurial skills so as to choose the right medium- to long-term priorities. It is precisely because it cannot fight on many fronts that it must find one single medium- to long-term priority. It must take great risks. Yet the most common mistake made by firms in short-term difficulties is to cut out all medium- and long-term expenditure or investment, with the excuse that it must concentrate entirely on its short-term problems. If this is applied indiscriminately to all its objectives, the future of the firm is easy to foresee. It will continue to limp along, with a new emergency every year, until finally it is a complete failure. At this point it will be forced to close. The reason for this inevitable fate is obvious. How could such a company be competitive two or three years ahead if it had invested nothing to achieve this competitiveness? Perhaps the market will be ready to halt for three years and wait for it? Certainly not! But then, if there is no sense in cancelling all investments in the future, reducing them all in proportion is also a losing strategy. The result would still be a mediocre firm, which could not survive for long in today's markets. The only valid solution for this firm is to have the courage to invest what little it has by concentrating on a single competitive factor on which to build the future. The choice is difficult, but also very important.

The final reference situation is the company which is highly profitable and in a strong leadership position (that is, with a strong advantage over its competitors). This situation can arise from the competitive advantage of having a product which the others do not have (product leadership) or because it is much better organized (for example, making what the customer needs very quickly to order) or through technological leadership. This type of firm can certainly afford the luxury of thinking more about the future than the present, particularly since it is running no risks for the next two or three years because of its privileged position. It should be thinking about what to do so that it will still be leader five or six years later, and should work intensively on these factors. If this firm started to squeeze its products intensively as a milked cow in the short-term, it would certainly make big profits today, but in a few years time would probably be in difficulty. It should therefore be dedicating its resources more to maintaining its position of leadership than to squeezing the maximum out of its competitive advantage.

In conclusion, the choice of objectives should be based on the following questions:

1   What volume of effort should I commit to each of the three management horizons (strategic mix)?

2   What are the priority objectives for the three horizons?

Confirmation that this is the way that world leaders already work comes from Rank Xerox, a top reference both in the USA (winner of the Malcolm Baldrige Quality Award) and in Europe (where Rank Xerox was winner of the first European Quality Award in 1992). It has defined its priority objectives as return on assets for the short term, market share for the medium term and customer and employee satisfaction for the long term.

The two operating objectives (return on assets (ROA) and market share) are carefully planned, launched and managed by the affiliates through the use of the Management by Policy and Policy Deployment mechanisms. The result of this deployment is the management operating plan. Returning to the effective planning process, for maximum operating effectiveness the ideal would be to have only one important objective each for the short and medium term, and a few policy guidelines for the long term. David T. Kearns, CEO of Rank Xerox, says a clear indication of the "major priority" can be of further help, but the reality is that we are going to have to supervise our objectives simultaneously (at least two operationally: the short and medium term). The problem then becomes how to manage and how to measure them. If we cannot decide on what is meant by improvement, how it is measured and supervised, and how we can ensure that it is taking place, we cannot talk about managing improvement. A Breakthrough plan for periods of special management usually has one to three priority objectives whose impact horizon is the short and short to medium term.

THE MULTI-YEAR INDICATORS

Another important aspect to consider in management by Breakthroughs is the choice and monitoring of the multi-year indicators. It is important to bear this aspect in mind to prevent the actions of the plan from being disconnected from the macroeconomic indicators that guarantee the continuation of the company's economic performance monitoring in time. The indicators are indispensable in evaluating the company's "state of health" year by year. Their task is to supervise the three management horizons mentioned, and are, thus, usually concerned with the economic results, the company's competitive level and the long-term security level.

An example of indicators to monitor and supervise in evaluating present and future performance is shown in Figure 3.3. While an example from Xerox America is shown in Figure 3.4.

CHOOSING THE OPERATIONAL LEVERS

Another important aspect to take into consideration when a Breakthrough plan is to be prepared is the choice of the areas in which to intervene. This choice, in fact, determines the type and the objectives of the actions to be planned. There are basically two types of lever to choose from: the operative causal lever and the organizational causal lever. Choosing the operative causal lever means identifying which aspects it is most productive to tackle in order to obtain the required results. A mistake I have often come across regards the nature of the actions, especially in their coherence with the time horizons of the objectives (Figure 3.5).

The following is an example which typifies this mistake:

A car manufacturing company had the objective of drastically improving the quality of its outgoing products; otherwise it risked a dangerous decline in its image in the short term, with consequent considerable negative impacts foreseen on its sales volumes. At the same time the company had started up a Total Quality programme aimed at improving its performance, product quality included. The most obvious decision seemed to be to concentrate the Total Quality programme massively on the priority "quality of the product already in production". As Total Quality for this company at the time was defined as "improvement programme through involvement", this meant activating a large number of improvement groups to work on the objective "quality". Another principle taken from Total Quality and culturally impelling, was that "quality must be built into the processes and not inspected in the finished product". So it was also considered a priority objective to reduce final testing activities. It was consequently decided to drastically reduce quality controls at the end of the production line and increase controls along the process. Result: the quality of the outgoing products actually

Indicators "by horizon"

Horizon	Priority	Indicator
Short (1–2 years)	Economic results	ROA
Medium (2–3 years)	Success in the market	Market share
Medium to long (3–5 years)	Confidence of success	Customer satisfaction
Long (beyond 5 years)	Company potential	Employee satisfaction

Figure 3.3   Example of "tableau de bord" for managing competitiveness.

Priority indicator	Objective (1990)	Goal ('91-'93)	Desired state (vision) ('93 +)
ROA	13.7% at corporate level - XCI 15.2% - XBRA 20.0% - XMEN 13.1% - REG.OPS 9.8%	20% at corporate level	Higher shareholders' return for an industry segment in *Fortune 500*
Market share	- XCI . . . % - XBRA . . . % -	Leadership in key business areas/ products	Market share leader (All targeted business areas and all op. co's)
Customer satisfaction	# 1 in all op. co's operative countries	Tracking to 100% satisfaction	All customers satisfied
Employee satisfaction	Improve employee satisfaction	Tracking to 100% satisfaction	All employees satisfied

Figure 3.4   *Example of multi-year plan (Xerox America).*

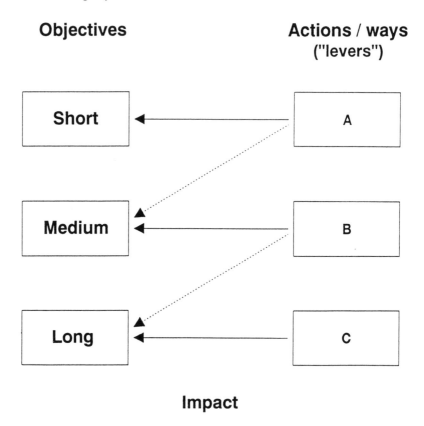

Figure 3.5   *Objectives – approaches: The coherence problem.*

worsened in the first months. It then improved slightly over the next two years but not enough for the market to become aware of the fact. The company went through two very hard years and lost market share as forecast.

What was the cause? Actions not adequately developed, perhaps? No. It was mistaken planning, due to the wrong approach. The objectives and the actions had been put together on time horizons that were "physically" impossible to match. Besides this there was an important requisite missing: the foundations on which to set and activate the actions for the future. In fact improvement programmes based only on group activities cannot produce Breakthrough results in the short term. This is a problem both of improvement volume in the chosen time span and of operative effectiveness. Furthermore, to obtain a drastic rise in the "quality capacity" of the processes, they must first go through a phase in which they are put under complete control. Lastly, the basis of improvement must always be the knowledge and supervision of the process capabilities and the cause-and-effect relations.

The correct approach would have been the following:

- Improve quality in the short term by intensifying the final inspection (a "Japanese" approach would have advised an obsessive 100% initial control)
- Improve quality in the medium term through an improvement plan to drastically reduce the defects registered in the short term by specific projects and raising the process capabilities (improvement plan and Statistical Process Control programme)
- Successive reduction of inspection activities
- Improve quality over the long term by revising design and industrial production methods, considering both the product and the process at the same time in order to guarantee adequate safety margins ("Robust Design" with release on the basis of relative process capability indices)

This programme of actions would undoubtedly have responded better to the car manufacturer's objectives.

Besides referring to the time horizon, the expression "causal lever" also refers to the cause-and-effect relation in the operating process. It means that we must try to ascertain exactly which operative causal factors can give us the required results. The question is then: "Which of the present operative performances must we improve to obtain the required results?" It means defining the practical means through which obtaining what we want. It will be a particularly useful examination because it will help us to avoid falling into the well-known managerial trap of wanting results and so managing everything "by results". A typical consequence of this approach would be the preparation of a plan of actions where the connections between the actions are quite clear – but only on paper! In practice it would simply be a plan of actions which "ought" to give the right results. What is missing from this type of plan? Quite simply, the operative connection!

There is no clear vision of what needs to be achieved operatively in the days and months to come to determine the conditions that will bring about the results required as the final outcome.

Let me describe a typical management plan "by results" which is unhelpful for operative management and is therefore ineffectual.

Suppose a company manufacturing cables wants to drastically reduce material "wastage". The accounts department says that the loss through waste is X million pounds' worth of rubber, Y million of PVC, Z million of copper, etc. The objective is to reduce such wastage by 30% in six months. The accounts department also advises that the best result should be obtained on the copper as it is the most costly material. According to the "results" approach, the natural deployment of the objective here would simply be to establish percentages of reduction in the consumption of the various materials and monitor them every month. Very often, alas, those who set the objectives forget to work out how they should be reached!

Despite the accountants' logic, the consumption of the materials in this particular process is actually greatly conditioned by one or more of the technical process phases, in which many metres of cable have to be rejected. In such a case an operatively workable plan would determine objectives and assign indicators and targets on the basis of the process phases. Such-and-such a percentage in phase A, so much per cent in phase B, etc. As there is usually a person responsible for each process phase, it would be a relatively simple matter to assign responsibility for these targets, whereas it would be much more difficult to identify those responsible for vague "improvement projects" (so they would be called) of "reduction in rubber wastage", "reduction in copper wastage", etc. Add to this some considerations on management. A monthly monitoring of material consumption, with only twelve checks a year, would be decidedly insufficient. It is far better to have daily monitoring or supervision (220 checks a year) of the loss of material, phase by phase and person by person. This permits a direct on-site evaluation of the results of the improvement actions.

Identifying causes and managing by causal levers, therefore, mean implementing a real operative management system that will produce real results instead of simply carrying out management controls on the results. An effective Breakthrough plan prefers real time management of causal performances rather than final monitoring of results (which still remain relevant, however, for management control).

Choosing the organizing causal levers means identifying the organizing methods with which to develop the planned actions. This, too, is an important and delicate aspect. Often objectives are not reached because the wrong method is chosen to tackle them. This is true both of the responsibilities and of the organizational forms. Quite frequently, for example, an interfunctional improvement group is assigned the objective of improving the operative performance of an activity that is already taking place. In such a case, "in-line management" by those responsible for the objective would be much more effective, especially regarding the time necessary to obtain the result. Consider, for example, the organizational aspects touched on by the imaginary case of the car manufacturer cited above, where it was thought that Breakthrough results would only be obtained through the activity of improvement groups.

There exists a considerable range of possible organizing methods to adopt. While a company taking its first steps in the world of improvement should not be too sophisticated in its choices, there is no doubt that some form of initial analysis should be made. In a more mature situation it will be quite natural to choose from various possible prepared approaches. The various possibilities are shown in Figure 3.6, while some examples are given in Figure 3.7.

THE OPERATIONAL PLAN

In its first version a Breakthrough operational plan that satisfies the requirements of effectiveness and coherence should (i) clearly identify the priority objectives and their impact horizons, (ii) define the right indicators to measure the results, (iii) identify the most effective causal levers (areas of intervention), (iv) define the operative indicators to be supervised and/or improved, (v) identify the relative targets, the plan of action and the organizational methods to achieve them. An example of such a plan is shown in Figure 3.8.

Impact horizon	Possible organizational levers
Short term (effects on operational performances in one year)	❑ "Crash" projects ❑ "Special" projects ❑ Campaigns ❑ Reorganization projects ❑ "Special" management by the line of operational performances ❑ ...
Medium term (effects on operational performances in 1–3 years)	❑ Changes in strategies ❑ Technical and methodological empowerment of personnel ❑ Technological projects ❑ Reorganization projects ❑ Special management by the line of process performances impacting on competitiveness ❑ ...
Medium to long term (effects on operational performances after 2–5 years)	❑ Changes in strategies ❑ Technological investments ❑ Reorganization projects ❑ Initiatives on culture, organization, skills ❑ ...

Figure 3.6   *Actions–objectives relationship.*

Figure 3.7   *Example of projects/actions.*

It contains a decidedly short-term oriented mix, with a priority action of re-set of the organization (people reduction). The medium-term objective also has considerable economic aspects (working capital), which is probably why it was chosen as the priority objective. Although the priorities are economic ones, due to short-term survival problems, the company also feels it should recover its competitiveness in the medium term so as to avoid needing another re-set in a few years time.

The potential loss of competitiveness is due to the company's customer service, which it is thought will reach a critical point in the scenario foreseen three to four years ahead. For this reason the company wants to improve its operative flexibility as well, while at the same time pursuing its cost reduction objectives (purchases and stocks). As may be seen, some of the objectives are quantitative; others are qualitative, which is a normal mix.

Impact	Objective	Indicator	Measurement unit	Target	Action (guidelines)	Ways
Short	□ Increase cash flow	Average positive cash flow	Millions ($)	+50 $ million (+40%)	□ Reduction of current stocks □ Increase of gross margin by changes in sales mix	Special management in line
Short	□ Fixed costs reduction in division "A"	Manpower Sub-indicators a. ..... b. ..... c.	N° OF PERSONS a. ..... b. ..... c.	-30% a. ..... b. ..... c.	□ General delayering □ Focus on factory "E"	"BPR" project
Medium	□ Reduction of total cost of purchased material □ Reduction of total supply Lead Time □ Reduction of raw materials stock	□ Specific indicators C=(a+b+c) □ Lead Time from order to delivery □ Working capital	$ ..... DAYS ..... $	-10% (...) -70% (...) -60% (...)	□ Total costs evaluations □ Elimination of inspection costs □ Integration of suppliers □ Direct deliveries in PULL	"BPR-Comakership" project

Figure 3.8   *Example of a Breakthrough plan.*

A double-barrelled measure has been chosen for the cash-flow objective: reduction of the current stocks, on the one side, and improvement of the gross margin through changes in the sales mix, on the other. In-line management has been chosen for these objectives, which means the company intends to intervene while maintaining the same structure, but drastically improving operative performances. With such an approach it is obvious that the best people to be responsible for reaching these targets are those who are managing those operations. It has been decided to implement real time Visual Management of the causal indicators of this objective.

Two asymmetrical operative priorities have been chosen for the "fixed costs reduction" objective – which is what any entrepreneur would do. In other words, the company has not worried about budgetary aesthetics, nor about overlapping or tallying the accounts. The approach chosen (Business Process Reengineering (BPR)) is clearly oriented towards innovative changes. The objective is to redesign the organization. There will be a reduction of both the management hierarchy structure and the people numbers in division A. Besides the BPR approach, there will also be a need for organizational know-how but, as we shall see later on, the rationale of the approach will be different. In both cases a work group will be set up which will have to complete its project (output, plan of operative actions) within two to three months. For the objectives "reduction of total cost of purchased materials", "reduction of total supply Lead Time" and "reduction of raw materials stocks", it will be necessary to adopt organizational know-how (BPR) but also specific strategic approaches (in this case Comakership). A study group is therefore set up (time available one month), subdivided into specific projects (two to six months). No causal indicators in Visual Management are planned for the "project" actions as this would be physically impossible. There will, however, be supervision, a control of action progress and a person responsible for progress and results. Much use will be made of co-responsibility situations.

4
Business Process Reengineering

In this chapter I will describe the methodology suggested for reorganizational actions. As I have already mentioned, the purpose of reorganizing is to improve those company performances that are most conditioned or determined by company organization. Their greatest impact is on the medium-term results (one to three years) because they are directed at improving a company's competitive capacity, the effects of which are generally felt after some time.

The reorganizing approaches adopted in recent decades have had the following characteristics:

- Prevalent emphasis on efficiency
- Focus on physical processes
- Strong lever on information processes

Another typical characteristic has been the conviction that reorganizing can be tackled almost entirely without analyzing the company's business factors, or that it can at least be carried on in parallel to the evolutions of business strategies. Evidence of this is the fact that even the related fields of know-how (including consultancy specializations) have developed almost independently. There are experts on organization, strategies, systems and functions, but we have realized by now that (i) organizing approaches must guarantee both maximum effectiveness and maximum efficiency at the same time, (ii) the processes with the greatest margins for improvement are not the physical ones but the management and clerical processes, (iii) manpower re-set action should be based on a clear preliminary definition of how core business process effectiveness would be maintained or raised. It has also been realized that reorganizing approaches should be global, providing both strategic and organizing contents.

The outcome of all these considerations is Business Process Reengineering (BPR), an approach that integrates method with content, and whose originality does not (or does only marginally) lie either in its methods or in its contents alone, but in its combination of both. Its rationale can be found in the fact that it tackles every organizational and operative problem through business process reasoning. This means, for example, that there is no point in optimizing the purchasing function by considering it on its own. It should only be dealt with in the context of the improvement of the whole supply process, which also involves many other company functions. This is the only way to appreciate which are the phases and activities without added value and which are the most critical aspects considering the operative objective of the process.

The same applies to all company processes, which should be examined through an approach whose major objective is the improvement of the core business processes – those which have the greatest impact on the company's business. In fact the first operative step in BPR is to identify the core business processes. Although this new approach is still very young, it has already been widely treated in the recent literature, in terms of both its innovative rationale and its organizing methodology approach. It is, however, the integration of the methodological aspects with the specific content aspects that makes BPR effective. This means, for example, that when redesigning a supply process it will be very important to support the process organizing criteria with specific advanced strategic contents such as Comakership.*

---

* See G. Merli, *Comakership*, Productivity Press, Cambridge 1992.

THE "BY PROCESS" APPROACH

In the most recent literature, the arguments that introduce the need to tackle reorganizing projects in this way are usually related to the following basic considerations: (i) managing and improvements have traditionally been tackled by functions while a company generates value through its processes not by its functions – it is the processes that create value; (ii) functional organization often generates management superstructures (specially central ones) and responsibility gaps in the interfunctional spaces; (iii) the greatest improvement potential is hidden within interfunctional organization (also because of point two).

Another consideration is that although it is true that most of the improvements necessary today concern performances connected with business processes (time to market, Lead Times, response capability, flexibility), it is absolutely impossible to obtain them with present organization which manages these processes by static, bureaucratic procedures, without introducing any direct operative managerial responsibility. It is thus unfortunately quite normal to find companies whose supply procedures, for example, are exactly the same as they were three years previously. They are only renewed every three to five years, when a management committee or a general manager asks the organization department to prepare and implement a new procedure to substitute the preceding one, which by then is clearly inadequate or has been ignored in practice (and which therefore needs to be updated). Such improvements are sporadic efforts introduced out of necessity, based on reorganizational projects managed by specialist staff groups. The operative management (line management) in the meantime manages the cost centres' performances "by budget", with only minimal attention to the interfunctional processes and to these reorganizational projects.

Once it has been decided that it is necessary to improve the process performances as a priority over those of cost centre, it is then vital to reorganize the company, give priority to the processes (BPR) and set up a coherent operative management (Management by Processes – Process Owners). It may generally be affirmed that the more Tayloristic the history of the company and the larger the central staff, the greater the beneficial effect of BPR. This beneficial effect is also generally greater in large companies, where the activities which are organizationally further away from the operating front (the processes, staff and support functions) can be brought back to a business-oriented rationale.

In order to deal with the subject on a more technical level, I think it may be helpful to state some preliminary definitions regarding the "by process" approach. A process is a series of activities that transforms inputs into outputs having value for the client for whom they are intended (internal or external). On a more technical level we might say that a process is a sequence of correlated activities aimed at a specific final result. The activities are repetitive, have added value, and need the contribution of human and information resources. (Figure 4.1).

Another useful definition is that of value of process output. A process output has greater value for the client if it is seen to have greater quality and/or a greater service capability, and if it occurs with lower costs and/or in a shorter time (Figure 4.2).

The following are some examples of processes with different values and therefore different impacts on company business; supplying materials, manufacturing, planning and scheduling, distributing/delivering products to customers, measuring product quality, measuring customer satisfaction, developing/processing new products, handling orders, selecting suppliers,

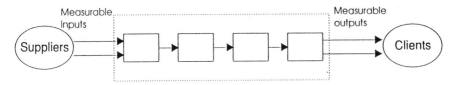

☐ *Sequence of activities that are correlated and finalized to a specific result*

- *Repetitive activities*
- *Adding value activities*
- *Resource consuming activities*

Figure 4.1   Process.

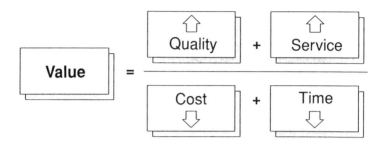

Figure 4.2   *Process value.*

monitoring the competition, training personnel, developing human resources, budgeting, maintaining management control, preparing accounts, evaluating investments, overseeing financial management, etc. As you can see, the definitions of processes are generally expressed by a verb (or activity) and an object. This emphasizes the type of added value generated and avoids confusion with the functions/offices that were responsible for part of these processes in the past. It is worth remembering here, in fact, that a supply process, for example, involves numerous functions (technical department, engineering, planning, purchasing, quality, incoming inspection, production, clients accounting, etc.). So the purchasing office only manages a small part of the process, normally that part which transforms a request for material into an order to the supplier.

Technically, a process is usually identified by using a flow diagram that shows its route and activities by the functions it passes through. An example of how the flow of a process ("order fulfilment") is mapped can be seen in Figure 4.3. An example of macro-mapping of all of a company's processes is shown in Figure 4.4.

The "by process" approach has five dimensions of possible activation:

1   The control dimension, supervising company's performances through process indicators (Activity Based Management)
2   The bottom-up improvement dimension, activating internal vendor–vendee chains for improvement along the processes (Daily Routine Work, (DRW) mechanisms)

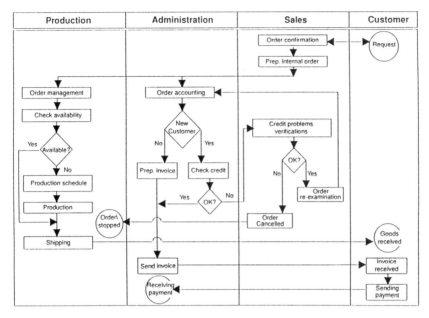

Figure 4.3 *"Map" of a business process (order fulfilment).*

3 The top-down systematic process improvement dimension, with the introduction of Management by Processes
4 The reorganizing dimension, using BPR
5 The managerial and organizational dimension, introducing "lean organization", with specific business, functional and process responsibilities

In this chapter I will be dealing with the reorganizing level, BPR, the only dimension able to produce organizational Breakthroughs in the short term. A synthesis of Managing by Processes and the internal vendor–vendee chains (Day to Day Management and DRW), can be found in Chapter 6. "Lean organization" by processes is dealt with in Chapter 9.

BUSINESS PROCESS REENGINEERING

According to Michael Hammer and James Champy, who may be considered the fathers of BPR, it consists of a "FUNDAMENTAL rethinking and RADICAL redesigning of business processes, to obtain DRASTIC IMPROVEMENTS in performance".

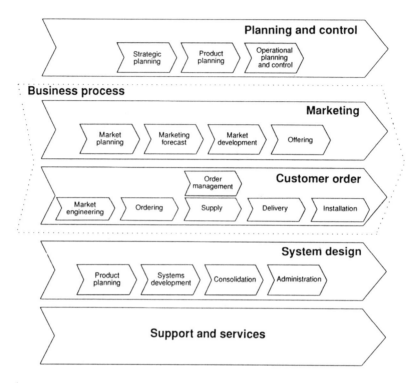

Figure 4.4   *Example of company processes mapping.*

The keywords "fundamental", "radical" and "drastic improvements" have very precise definitions:

1 *Fundamental:* rethinking the process eliminating all preconceived ideas, ignoring the present configuration of the process, thinking only about what it should be like (to obtain the desired performance)
2 *Radical:* going back to the origins and acting on the basic levers; reinventing, not just improving by modifying what already exists
3 *Drastic improvements:* not being satisfied with improvements of 10%; making Breakthroughs or quantum leaps

A BPR approach should, of course, concentrate on the most important processes. There is a general rule-of-thumb reference that defines company processes by dividing them into two categories: the core business primary processes and the supporting processes.

The core business or primary processes, which have the greater impact on the company's business results, are often characteristic of the sector in which the company operates, they create a "value" that the client recognizes and in general they are fundamental to obtaining success. They are normally limited to a maximum of five to eight in number.

The following is a list of examples of core business processes for various types of industry:

1   *Production to order:* proposal preparation, design and engineering, order management, purchasing, components production, assembling, transportation, installation, etc.
2   *Mass-production:* Research and Development (R&D), design, engineering, purchasing, production, distribution, sales, technical assistance, etc.
3   *Trading and marketing business:* client satisfaction monitoring, market research, marketing, purchasing, distribution, promotion, sales, assistance, complaints management, etc.

The support processes are the ones necessary for the management but they are without any added value for the product/service recognized by the client. These are the processes that should be eliminated when a way can be found "not to need them". Take the example of the production scheduling offices "pensioned off" by the Kanban systems. Once the way to make them unnecessary had been found they were eliminated because a scheduling office is a management requirement, not a value added to the product. The following is a list of examples of support processes: materials management, planning, maintenance, quality control, productivity control, strategic planning, budgeting, management control/cost accounting, "safety and environment" management, financial administration, human resources management, human resources development and investment management. Figure 4.5 shows an example of core business processes and support processes individuated by a "white" appliances manufacturer.

BPR intervention means designing and setting up an operative configuration of the process which is significantly different from the previous one and provides considerably better performance. Figure 4.6 shows an example of the result of a BPR approach, giving a before-and-after comparison between the two operational configurations. It is the spare parts management process of a company manufacturing big engines.

The operative results of this reengineering are the following:

- The stages necessary have passed from 17 to 12
- The number of functions involved has dropped from seven to four
- The average number of days required for fulfilling a domestic order has dropped from 21 to 2.7 (87%)
- The average number of days required for fulfilling a foreign order has dropped from 36 to 6.7 (82%)

The main actions taken in this case concern organizational aspects alone and can be summarized as the elimination of operations without added value and the "paralleling" of operations

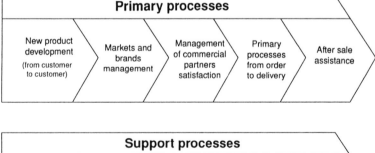

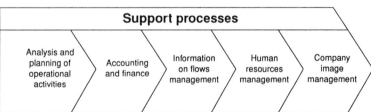

Figure 4.5 *Primary and support processes identified by a company operating in the white appliances sector.*

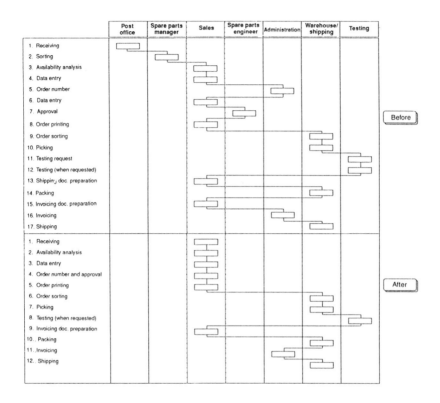

Figure 4.6 *Spare parts management.*

without added value but necessary for management. How these actions were identified will be briefly illustrated in the section entitled "Designing the vision".

BPR METHODOLOGY

BPR approach has already produced more "schools" of approach. This is due to the fact that it has generated considerable volumes of consultancy work (in the USA two out of three companies say they have introduced it), so the various consultancy firms have had to develop their own ways of presenting it, and some companies have decided to organize their old approaches under the new label of BPR. It is also true that much of what is used by the BPR approaches previously existed as know-how. It may therefore also be affirmed that BPR is a new formal way of dressing and presenting already known approaches. Although much of the methodological content is not innovative, the general approach definitely is.

These innovative elements are basically (i) the preliminary identification of the core business processes, (ii) the definition of the performance indicators of these processes and (iii) the design of their "visions". In other words the methods by which the desired configuration is designed are innovative. The methodology used by Galgano & Associates is shown in Figure 4.7.

CHOOSING PRIORITIES AND TARGETS

Priorities are normally chosen after some form of benchmarking (comparison with competitors' performances) has been carried out. Indeed it is a company's competitive position that is the decisive factor in whether or not to carry out or to orient an organizational revision in the BPR rationale. The other factor that can spur such a decision is the acknowledgement that the company's overall performance is not satisfying the financial expectations. This sort of situation often gives rise to structure cost reduction actions.

For the Breakthrough approach illustrated in this book, the departure point is the identification of an improvement objective on the company's performance in a specific aspect. On a practical level, however, benchmarking is always important. In fact if the objective concerns a need to align the company's position with the best competitors, it will be very important to examine their performance and the methods with which they execute the related business processes, in order to identify where the operative improvements can be planned. If the objective is to significantly outdo the competition, then the improvement ideas cannot be looked for in their processes. They must be found by examining the best processes in the world, which will presumably be found in other sectors. These do not necessarily have to be technologically or organizationally more sophisticated. If a TV or PC manufacturer wanted to drastically improve his or her

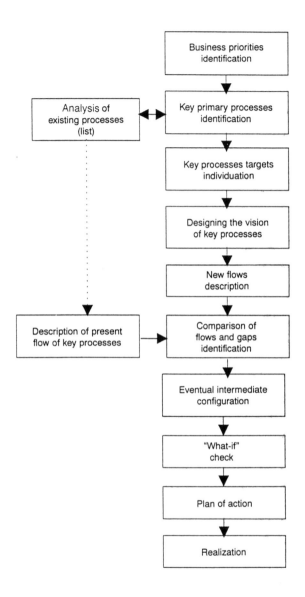

Figure 4.7 *Business Process Reengineering.*

distribution process, he or she would have to look for innovative
ideas among the best executors of that same process, for example
among fresh food distributors. These companies, for purely

physical reasons, must have found effective and efficient operating methods both for rapid distribution and for keeping their stocks low.

Analyses of this sort, conducted outside one's own sector, are at the heart of real benchmarking.

The output of a benchmarking activity is always the definition of a business performance objective. The following are examples of targets identified in this way:

- 70% improvement in product quality
- 90% improvement in service level
- 50% reduction in customer complaints
- 50% reduction in order fulfilment times
- 50% increase in flexibility
- 30% reduction in structure costs

Statements like these are definitions of intervention priorities and their relavant targets.

CHOOSING PRIORITY PROCESSES AND OPERATIONAL TARGETS

Once the objectives we want to achieve have been defined, we must identify which processes to tackle (or start from scratch) to transform our objectives into results. The processes will be decisive in achieving the results. In 80% of cases the task is relatively simple. The other cases need rather more sophisticated cause-and-effect analyses. However usually one to three priority processes to reengineer will be identified. There is only one exception to this rule: the case in which the objective is to reduce structure costs. Here it will be necessary to examine all the processes and the criterion with which to choose the priorities will in this case be the separation of the core business processes from the support processes. The next step is to identify the improvements to achieve on those processes to guarantee the required result. This means finding indicators with which to measure process performances and the relative improvement targets necessary to guarantee objective performance (Figure 4.8.).

The output of an analysis of this type can be shown through the following example:

1 Company performance objective: 30% reduction in time to market
2 Connected priority processes: designing and industrialization
3 Processes target:
   - Designing time (from concept to prototype): –20%
   - industrialization time: –50%
   - constraints: quality new products = present quality, total cost of process (resources) 15% lower than at present

DESIGNING THE "VISION"

This is perhaps the most important phase of the whole BPR process. By vision we mean the operative image of the process we want to set up, that is the procedural configuration of the new process. Three types of reference are used to design the vision:

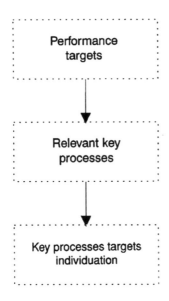

Figure 4.8 *Key processes target individuation.*

1   The operative targets identified in the preceding phase
2   The general organizational criteria (organizing by processes, lean organization, micro-organizational principles, elements of managerial culture)
3   The specific strategic and organizational principles of the process to be reengineered

These ingredients are combined together operatively as in the scheme in Figure 4.9. If the priority objective is to improve a process performance, the reorganization will be tackled starting from the specific strategic principles of that process (on the right of the figure). Then necessary testing will be carried out with the general organizational principles (on the left of the figure). If the priority objective is the reduction of structure costs, the method must be followed in the opposite direction, starting from the left side, applying the general organizational principles and then reiterating tests with the specific process principles. The following are some syntheses of the contents of such references.

General Organizing Criteria

1   Organizing by processes:
   - Priority to the core business processes
   - Nomination of people responsible for the processes (Process Owners)
   - Organization of the support processes "in pull" (serving the core business processes)
   - Operative decentralization (to the lowest possible levels) of the support processes
2   Lean organization:
   - Delayering (reduction of the number of managerial levels)
   - Shortening the structure (reduction of horizontal fragmentation along the process)
   - Widening of responsibilities (broadening control range)
3   Micro-organization:
   - Job enrichment (reconstruction of global tasks)
   - Job enlargement (along the process)
   - Flexible and inter-changeable roles along the process
   - Elimination of activities with no added value
   - Team work

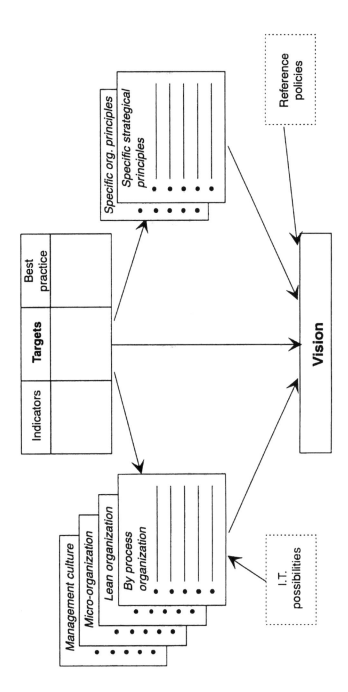

Figure 4.9   *Designing the "vision"*

4   Managerial culture:
   • Managerial priority to flows and processes
   • Global flow responsibilities
   • Operative and decisional delegation
   • Coherency of authority levels with reponsibility levels
   • Entrepreneurship

Figure 4.10 shows an example of BPR using the above types of organizing principle. It was prepared for a company manufacturing small customized plants. The process tackled was order fulfilment. The number of people involved in the process fell from 78 to 33, and programming times dropped from 2.5 weeks to just 2.5 days. The general organizing criteria used were the following:

• Aggregation of responsibility on the process (from three first level responsibilities to one)
• Delayering (reduction of the number of hierarchical levels)
• Widening of roles along the process
• Elimination of duplication and reworks
• Reduction of document transfers

Specific Process Principles (Organizing and Strategic)

These specific principles concern the different business processes separately. There are principles for the manufacturing process, for the development of new products, for distribution, purchasing, sales, management control, etc. They are in effect combinations of specific strategic approaches and general organizing principles, individualized for each single process. The following are examples of specific strategic approaches:

1   Production: Lean Production/Total Manufacturing Management, Total Productive Maintenance, Total Industrial Engineering
2   Supplies: Comakership, Partnership
3   Distribution: Total Logistic Strategy, Supply Chain Management
4   Product development/designing: Forward Engineering, Simultaneous/Concurrent Engineering, Design for Manufacturing/Assembling; Codesign

Order processing/production planning process

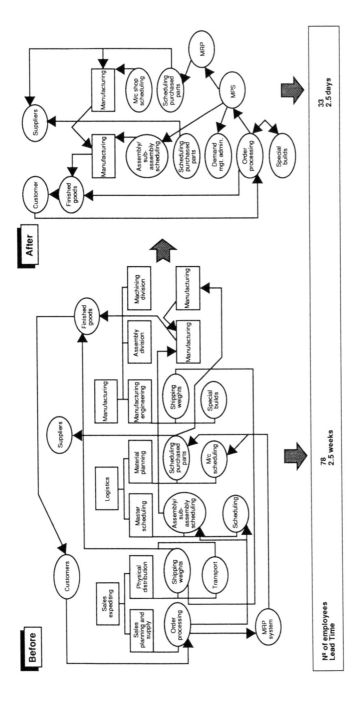

Figure 4.10   *Capital equipment manufacturer. (Source: Coopers & Lybrand)*

As previously stated, these principles are combined with the general reference organizing principles. There is a synthesis of some specific strategic process approaches in Chapter 6.

Another reference is given by the specific process indicators. These are used to establish targets for benchmarking and for measuring improvements. An example of a reference scheme that includes all the ingredients mentioned above is shown in Figure 4.11. The process involved is that of new product development.

Figure 4.12 shows an example of a BPR project using a reference scheme similar to the one shown in Figure 4.10, but applied to a procurement process. The company concerned operates in the electro mechanical sector. It has a customized production, using machine tools and assembling, although its products are made up of fairly standardized components. As can be seen, the process phases have dropped from eight to four and the number of functions involved from three to two (with the same structure).

The main criteria used were:

- Reduced fragmentation of the process (from eight to four phases)
- Speeding up of decision processes
- Elimination of the operations with no added value (e.g. sending the order to the supplier)
- Adoption of Comakership

It was the last of these ingredients that enabled the operative procedure to be so revolutionized. It meant eliminating the need to prepare internal purchasing requests and to send orders to the suppliers at every supply. These were substituted with general contracts and deliveries were automatic, in pull. It was activated and managed directly by the core business process of engineering and production.

THE ACTION PLAN

Once the vision of the new process has been designed and the operative macro-procedures identified, a comparison is made with the ones. Through this comparison we can identify the

Specific organizational principles	Specific strategic principles	Reference indicators	Target
⊓ Simultaneous/ concurrent engineering	⊓ Customer orientation (QFD)	⊓ Time to market	
		⊓ Development cost	
	⊓ Codesign	⊓ N°/cost of necessary modifications	
⊓ Project management	⊓ Carry over		
⊓ Twin career paths (managers, professionals)	⊓ Shelf-engineering	⊓ % of carry over	
⊓ Process integration for customer (QFD)	⊓ Standardization	⊓ % of standard components	
⊓ Co-location	⊓ Last phase product differentiation ("mushroom concept")	⊓ Warranty costs	
	⊓ Global make or buy	⊓ Hours per product developed	
	⊓ Comakership	⊓	

Figure 4.11 Process: New product development

gaps existing. They may be of various types: physical layout, technology, professional capacities, systems, managers' roles, organization, etc. With the entrepreneurial approach put forward in this book, it is suggested that the most critical of these gaps – and the most difficult to bridge – be identified. It will then become the departure point from which to choose the methods with which the process of applying the vision will be chosen. It would not be entrepreneurial to start up indiscriminately all the actions at the same time. That would mean subtracting resources from the critical action pathways and priorities. It would also involve investments and effort which could not be immediately transformed into improvements because they would be made ineffective by the absence of the main link. It is the most important and most critical actions which must set the pace for all the others. Therefore the action plan must be priority driven or constraint driven.

Analyzing the actions necessary for the most critical pathways means deciding between two options: either attaining the vision in a single jump or falling back on an approach that uses one or more intermediate phases. If the second option is chosen an intermediate evolutionary configuration will have to be defined and it must be carried out during a first design and executive

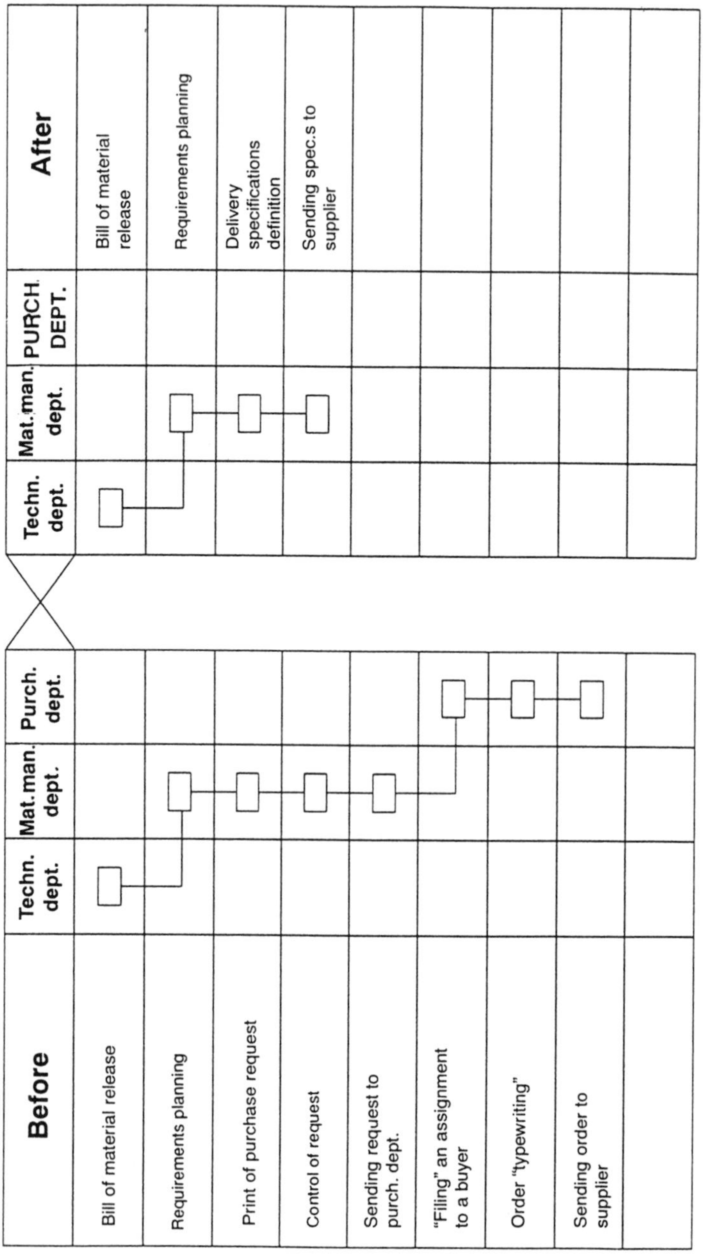

Figure 4.12 Process: Procurement/supplying.

phase. It must guarantee significant results in the short term and in the right direction to attain the vision. My suggestion is that pathways that do not provide rapid operative results be avoided.

The priority-driven or constraint-driven action plan must pragmatically include actions on the other gaps, sufficient to support the critical pathway. I suggest these actions should not be overdone because for the time being it would be a waste of effort, giving little leverage. It must be decided which, if any, exceptions are to be made and this should be decided by entrepreneurial reasoning. However, before launching an action plan, of whatever type, it is good policy to do a "what if" test. This means checking upstream whether the planned actions will really be able to obtain the required results and applying cause-and-effect evaluations. If the *constraints theory* approach is well known in the company it could be very useful to construct a "future reality tree". The action plan will contain a mix of interventions of the types described and the relative programme of operative actions, with the relative deployment.

"DELAYERING" THROUGH A BPR APPROACH

To aid in the understanding of the practical application of BPR, I will illustrate a real case, a delayering project, carried out through a "lean organization" rationale aimed at the reduction of hierarchical levels and management complexity. The project was designed for a plant with 2000 people, belonging to a mechanical company. The objectives were identified by benchmarking the best leaders in the industry and in other sectors. They were chosen by positioning the company on an intermediate level among the best competitors and world leaders in other sectors. The indicators and related planned improvements were the following:

- Number of managerial layers from five to three
- Span of operative control from 15 to 30
- Span of hierarchical control from four to 7.5
- Organizational "centre of gravity" from 4.1 to 2.5

The number of managerial layers means the hierarchical levels along the longest path, starting from the factory manager (included) down to the lowest operational–blue collar level (excluded). The span of operative control means the ratio of total number of workers to number of heads coordinating them, while the span of hierarchical control is the average value of the structure hierarchical references, taking into consideration all the managerial and operative coordination positions (thus excluding the manual workers). Managerial position means the management of persons and/or function responsibility (including positions without subordinates), and/or responsibility for company resources (financial, information system, etc.) and/or for results.

The management centre of gravity is the ratio between the summation of the products "number of positions of the hierarchical level × distance in levels from the top" and "total number of managerial positions". These are conventional indicators, chosen to plan and monitor the improvements. The project process used is shown in Figure 4.13. The results of the project were equal to or better than the targets.

A COMPREHENSIVE BPR APPROACH

I will illustrate a case of global reorganizational Breakthrough, where the first phase is only based on reorganizational actions. In traditional terms this type of project would be called a "reorganization project" or "company restructuring". It could still be called this but it is presented as a BPR project because the approach, in this case, was decidedly unconventional.

In a classical reorganizing approach, once the strategic priorities had been defined, a new organizational structure would be formulated as the first step (the new organization chart). Then the operational procedures would be developed. With the BPR approach, first, core business processes related to the strategic priorities are identified, followed by the procedures for executing and managing them and, as a last step, comes the definition of the best structure for the operative management of the new organization. The design of the organization chart is only the formality concluding the project.

The priority objective of BPR is to make the company's processes work better, making the company more competitive.

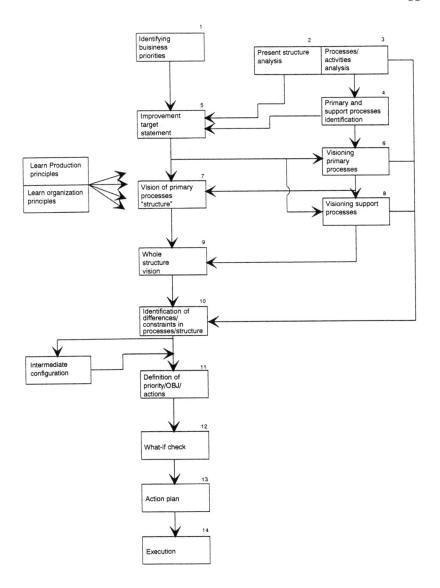

Figure 4.13 *Designing the new organization.*

The organizational structure is only an instrument in the service of the processes ("upside-down pyramid"). It is certainly not easy to challenge this approach! The development of the project is reiterative, so management and process organization interact repeatedly in the definition of the operative procedures. But the different entry point sometimes produces very different conclusions.

For the consultant whose job it is to approach structure projects, the BPR methodology is far more objective and sustainable. It is hard for me to forget the difficulties I have seen in my working experience, when the advantages and disadvantages of two alternative structures had to be compared. Everything seemed relative and easy to challenge when it was a case of simply comparing two reference organization charts. It is much easier to follow a logical reasoning which leads up to the definition of the organization and the structure only as a final conclusion. At this point any alternatives will consider only very limited spheres.

The following example concerns a large multi-division electromechanical company and I will illustrate the approach used and the conclusions reached:

The background elements that suggested the adoption of a global BPR approach were the following:

1 *The company had already tried in the past to improve the performance of its processes through a Total Quality programme but without success. Total Quality had not helped to provide the 30–50% improvement in times and quality that the company required.*
2 *It would therefore not have been expedient to use Total Quality methodologies and terms in the first phase of the reorganization so as not to recall programmes that had failed in the past.*
3 *It was decided to proceed with a global revision to fill in some potentially dangerous gaps compared with the competition and to tackle all the important processes.*
4 *It was necessary to achieve big results fast (Breakthroughs).*
5 *The revision of the organization of the operative divisions had to take place under company direction for the sake of managerial coherence and cultural evolution.*

On the basis of these background elements the following approaches and ingredients were identified:

1 *The need to develop a coherent reorganization under company direction meant that a company development reference model had to be*

predefined, containing the reference policies for managing the strate-
gic and operative coherences of the changes.

2 *The types of improvement expected were related to process perfor-*
mances. A "by process" approach was therefore obligatory (BPR).

3 *The extent of the improvements expected compared to the competi-*
tion imposed a careful benchmarking and challenging objectives
(Breakthroughs).

4 *The rapidity of the results required imposed quick results and con-*
crete outputs.

The project was therefore based on three elements: the company reference model; BPR methodology; and challenging objectives. The approach is shown as a logical flow in Figure 4.14 (see p. 56). The scheme, however, needs some clarification.

The framework of the project is composed of the logical flow of the BPR. The process is activated on the basis of reference business targets, defined after benchmarking competitors. It was a straightforward comparison of output performances (times, quality, cost, innovation level, service level) to identify the objectives to pursue.

The output performance objectives lead to the identification of the primary processes and the relative sub-objectives (see the section on BPR in this chapter). The primary processes so defined are put into the company development reference model to carry out the relative deployment of the reference policies. The reference model is a grid where plans are laid out for the development policies of the primary processes and the management and company cultural capabilities necessary to make such developments possible and coherent.

An example of such a model (only filled in for the primary processes) is shown in Figure 4.15 (see pp. 58-60). It forms the source of strategic and coherency aims in constructing the vision of the integrated model of the company processes. Another benchmarking took place to construct the vision of the single processes. Worldwide best practices were looked for also in other sectors. The time scale employed was the following:

• The integrated model of the primary processes was tackled in the first three months

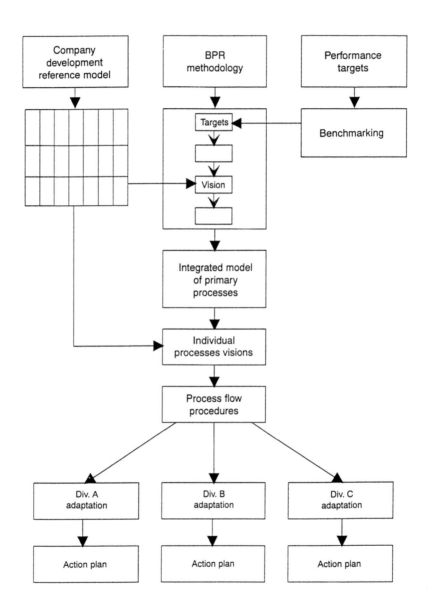

Figure 4.14   *Global BPR approach.*

- Division adaptation required approximately two months
- Operative execution started up five months from the beginning

All the new operative procedures in the primary processes were activated within 12 months. The primary processes identified were: designing, engineering, purchasing, manufacturing. The operational plan is shown in Figure 4.16 (see p. 61).

Dvlpt. Phases	Organization & Culture				Primary Processes			Business Strategy
	Org.	Cult.	Human Res.	M'gmt. Style	Design and Engineering	Supplies	Manufacturing	
Today					– Process broken up into various functions/specializations – Integration by rules/procedures and coordination systems – Sector optimization for design, purchases/repetitive manufacturing – Redesigning for each order – Emphasis on standardization of the components alone	– Centralized purchasing, fragmented supply process – Large number of traditional suppliers – Best price priority – Undifferentiated approach/tenders – Supplier evaluation not systematic – Acceptance control	– Rigid production system – Integration by programming systems – Research of efficiency by specific subsystems (priority on resource/productivity saturation) – Priority on direct costs; unequal costs supervision – Recourse to buffer stocks – Little attention to internal client satisfaction/no coordination in satisfying external customers	

Figure 4.15   The company grid.

Dvlpt. Phases	Organization & Culture				Primary Processes			Business Strategy
	Org.	Cult.	Human Res.	M'gmt. Style	Design and Engineering	Supplies	Manufacturing	
Phase 1					– Functions grouped by common product and process objectives – Concurrent engineering (timely involvement of all those involved in the process, internal and external) – Integrated product development groups (multi-sector/multi-speciality) – Design development for manufacturing and assembling – Design review – Identification and evaluation of distinctive key factors – Identification of modular systems	– Coherent management of relations with suppliers (technical, economic, programming) – Purchasing marketing – Limited number of suppliers – System of supplier evaluation – Emphasis on improvement of global cost of supplies/Lead Time/quality: supplies by groups – Introduced codesign – Planning supplier relationships by analysis of strategic value – Price/cost analysis – Orientation to Comakership – Self-certification by strategic suppliers	– Job rotation/multivides workers – Emphasis on global efficiency as supervision of priority costs – Opening processes to outside (integration with suppliers) – Identification and first reduction of waste – Reduction of Lead Time and flow focus – Reduction of stocks (WIP, warehouse) – Greater awareness of internal client/coordination outside customer satisfaction management – Activating process capability management	

Figure 4.15 *contd.*

Dvlpt. Phases	Organization & Culture				Primary Processes			Business Strategy
	Org.	Cult.	Human Res.	M'gmt. Style	Design and Engineering	Supplies	Manufacturing	
Phase 2					- Simultaneous engineering paralleling internal activities with suppliers in codesign - Technical memory set up - Quality function deployment adoption - Management of distinctive key factors as a function of market dynamics - Extension of system modularization	- Systematic evaluation, classification and selection of suppliers (global costs/Lead Time/quality/process capability) - Continuous improvement programmes (supplier value chain) - Widespread codesign - Comakership for critical supplies - Strategic integration with selected (partnerships) - Widespread self-certification	- Process supervision and flow / lean organization - Systematic elimination of waste - Short, reliable times - Integrated and flexible logistical management (WIP, warehouses, suppliers) for mix variation - Total productive maintenance - Priority on internal client/outside customer satisfaction	
Phase 3 (Vision)					- Integrated process - Dynamic, market driven process organization - Dynamic integration with outside development - Modular system designing	- Integrated value chain management (suppliers, company, customers) - Dynamic, differentiated approach to second level suppliers (self-certification, logistical integration, codesign, Comakership, partnership)	- Market driven, short factory - Productive system flexible for mix variation - Flow production	

Figure 4.15 contd.

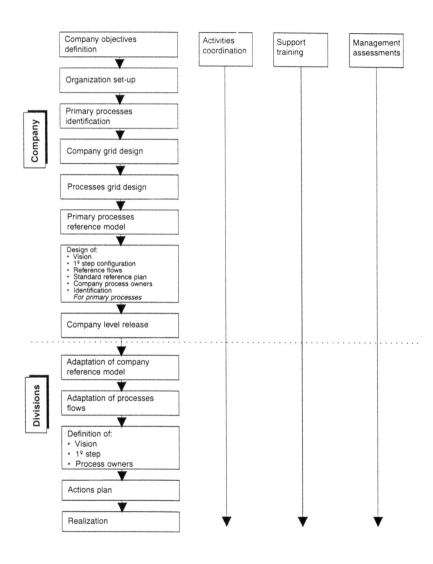

Figure 4.16   *Global BPR operational plan.*

5
Specific Approaches

In this chapter I will give a synthesis of the process-specific strategic and organizational principles previously referred to in Chapter 4 on Business Process Reengineering (BPR). I will deal with them separately for two reasons: first, so as not to complicate the presentation of the BPR rationale, and secondly, because the principles have an objective, autonomous value (in some cases even greater than the BPR approach itself). They are the accumulation of the best applications worldwide of the related company processes. I have chosen the most important:

- Lean Production
- Total Logistic Strategy
- Comakership
- Concurrent Engineering

LEAN PRODUCTION

This strategic principle is the synthesis of the approaches to production developed by Japanese industry throughout the 1960s, 1970s and 1980s. They have been adopted by Western companies since the 1980s.

The Lean Production principle may be seen as the sum of three specific approaches:

1 *Total Manufacturing Management (TMM)*. This emphasizes the organizational aspects of production.
2 *Total Industrial Engineering (TIE)*. This underlines the type of approach and contribution that human resources must have in the spheres of production;
3 *Total Productive Maintenance (TPM)*. This concentrates on machinery management.

Total Manufacturing Management

The strategic and organizational principles of TMM/Lean Production have been set up on the basis of developments in applications derived from the Toyota Production System. They can be briefly defined in six basic statements (the organizational principles of TMM):

1 *Just in time (JIT)*. Producing finished goods just in time to deliver them, producing semi-finished items and sub-assemblies just in time to assemble them, resupplying with purchased supplies just in time to use them.
2 *Stockless production*. From maximum energy management (as much inventory as may be needed to cover problems) to minimum energy management (as much inventory as may be needed to identify problems).
3 *Preventing waste*. Nothing more than the right quantities of materials, parts, space and work time that are indispensable for adding value to products.
4 *Flow production*. Comparable to a chemical pipeline process, which proceeds from raw materials to a finished product, without interruptions, unnecessary handling or intermediate inventory.
5 *Pull system*. From production that determines the flow of materials to a flow of materials that determines production.
6 *Dynamic responsibility*. From static, phase responsibility to dynamic responsibility according to the flow.

The Value of the Production Flow

The six principles illustrate the importance of production flow for the TMM approach. A special indicator termed flow value has been created for this specific purpose. It is widely used to compare flow levels in firms operating within the same market sector, or to analyze improvements within the same firm (flow value is a relative indicator).

Flow value can be universally applied to all production processes. It is defined as the ratio between average production Lead Time and net manufacturing time required for producing a single unit of a given product. The emphasis on production flow is operationally supported through the use of indicators that have been developed for determining the efficiency of production flows. Their use is becoming increasingly widespread; in many instances, they are entirely or partially replacing traditional indicators, which are based solely upon efficiency in terms of resources. In fact, use of an operational model where the priorities are inverted compared to those of the past, is becoming more common. Whereas it was customary, several years ago, to manage efficiency within individual units on a day-to-day basis, with periodic evaluation of logistical efficiency, the opposite is now becoming normal. In other words, logistical efficiency is managed on a day-to-day basis, and production efficiency is evaluated periodically. The indicators employed are extremely varied, depending significantly upon production categories. As no satisfactory "comprehensive" indicators are available, it is necessary to rely upon the simultaneous use of multiple indicators intended for evaluating various logistical factors. Some of these indicators are cited in Figure 5.1

A firm preparing to transform its production structure into TMM must, after it has assimilated the indispensable participation principle, decide where to begin. In fact, a model as comprehensive as TMM offers many possible access points, all of which are synergistically interrelated. However, different categories of production, different phases in the evolution of companies, and the critical nature or appropriateness of specific points in time call for extremely specific and carefully chosen points of access. From a theoretical standpoint, it is possible to identify 17 possible criteria. These are TMM's 17 organizing points, and they are listed in Figure 5.2.

The first 12 points pertain specifically to organization of production. Points 13 and 14 pertain to quality, while 15 and 16 relate to manufacturing engineering, and point 17 addresses

CLIP Committed Line Item Performance (reliability of production)

$$CLIP = \frac{\text{Number of items implemented in orders}}{\text{Number of items in orders confirmed by production}} \times 100\%$$

MTT Manufacturing Throughput Time (organizing efficiency of the process)

$$MTT = \frac{\text{WIP value}}{\text{Value of daily output}} = \text{... days}$$

Stock ratio (financial value of production)

$$SR = \frac{\text{Total value of stock (warehouse + WIP)}}{\text{Average Daily Use}} = \text{... days}$$

CSL Customer Service Level (organizational efficiency)

$$CSL = \frac{\text{Number of complete orders delivered on time}}{\text{Total number of orders confirmed to clients}} \times 100\%$$

VDP Vendor Delivery Performance

$$P\% = 100 - \frac{\text{Number of items in order completed with a delay}}{\text{Total number of items in orders}}$$

PD Ratio

$$PD\ Ratio = \frac{\text{Total Lead Time}}{\text{Required delivery time}}$$

Schedule adherence early–on time–late "charts"

DT Distance travelled

MSE Master schedule execution

$$PDM\% = \frac{(\text{Number of units produced - unscheduled units produced}) \times 100}{\text{Total number of units produced}}$$

Turnover

$$T = \frac{\text{Estimated yearly production volume}}{\text{Average volume of total stocks}}$$

Figure 5.1   *Logistical indicators.*

1. Lead Time reduction

2. Flow production

3. Short/parallel lines/group technology

4. Levelled production

5. Management by bottlenecks

6. Flow balance/synchronized production

7. Flexible/frequent/continuous scheduling

8. Pull control (Kanban)

9. Visual Control System (VCS)

10. Stockless production

11. Jidohka

12. Set-up time reduction

13. In process control

14. Quality improvement

15. Pre-automation and autonomation

16. Cost curves

17. Mushroom concept

Figure 5.2   *The 17 organizing points of Total Manufacturing Management.*

product design. It is not possible to prepare generalized approach models because, as indicated previously, models are determined more by respective situations than by production categories. In terms of indicating the practicability and the priority of the preceding points on the basis of production categories alone, the following general framework is nevertheless valid.

Repetitive Manufacturing Production (Distinct Products)

All of the 17 points are applicable and relevant to repetitive manufacturing production. Nevertheless, it is advisable to choose from among the first 14 points for an approach to the first step.

Repetitive Production by Order (Standard Products, with only Production by Order)

Group technology (3), synchronized production (6), set-up (12) and the mushroom concept (17) are especially relevant to repetitive production by order; possibilities with "pull" control may also be applicable. Today, Kanban control is used for producing small numbers of items per year – for example, in machine tool production. This means that several other of the 17 points may be valid.

"Batch" production (production by lots). Granting priority to stockless production (10), set-up (12) and the mushroom concept (17) is recommended for batch production, but none of the other points should be dismissed.

Process production ("continuous" product). The best access points to process production are stockless production (10), set-up (12) and process control (13), but the mushroom concept (17) and autonomation (15) are highly effective in some cases.

Pure customized production (specific products for specific clients). This category of production is usually inappropriately overlooked by JIT, precisely because it was the building industry that launched the JIT era in Japan. A significant transformation can be introduced, with exceptional economic gains in some instances, by using an approach based on cost curves (16), in conjunction with set-up (12), the mushroom concept (17). At the same time, bottleneck approach (5), Visual Control System (VCS) (9) and quality (14), should not be overlooked.

A further organizational criterion of Lean Production is synchronized production. In situations where controlled production has not yet been introduced or where high numbers or diversification of sub-assemblies exist, a Kanban inventory of even a few minutes would generate an unsupportable cost. Thus, it is necessary to rely upon synchronized production, which is actually an outgrowth of Kanban systems.

In more precise terms, there are two ways of evolving beyond Kanban:

1   By developing comprehensive flows without disruption of continuity (pipelines, without a need for linkage through self-regulating circles or Kanbans)
2   By avoiding the need to wait for removal signals from a given location in order to start production upstream, whereby production must be activated by an advance requirements signal

The first objective can be pursued through complete flow production lines, the second is accessible through the introduction of synchronized systems. Synchronized production is already extensively employed in the car industry, particularly in areas where it is physically impossible to maintain hourly inventories, because the components are either too large (seats, for example) or too expensive (engines, for example). The system is based on rapid transmission of information originating at the beginning of an assembly line. The following example pertains to car seats.

For seats, precise assembly requirements (types, colours and sequence) become known only at the moment when automobile bodies are placed upon the line (after painting). At this point, a sensor reads a Kanban/bar code and transmits the relevant information to the unit where seats are produced (in this instance, a supplier), which is then given two hours to produce them (as he or she, too, holds no stocks) in the specified sequence, according to a predetermined rate and volume (for example, 12 sets of seats which are equivalent to 12 minutes of production or to 12 cars). In this instance, two types of production (car assembly and seat production) are synchronized. Use of these techniques for repetitive production in a job shop factory – where different situations generate different forms – is less extensive. In such cases, synchronization is referred to the management of bottlenecks, that occurs through scheduling with a Materials Requirement Planning (MRP) methodology, whereas operational synchronization of production flows (according to a sufficient capacity) is controlled by pull–Kanban systems. In complex job shop environments, reliance upon systems derived from the Theory of Constraints may be extremely useful.

The purpose of these systems is to achieve control of the work pace and flow rhythm by means of bottlenecks within processes, with application of the following principles:

1   Scheduling of work in relation to bottlenecks is based upon market demand.
2   The schedule for subsequent operations is determined by bottleneck output (constraint).
3   The schedule for any prior operations is determined on a pull basis, by the inventory that supplies the respective bottleneck ("any" because this theory should try to use the first work stage as the real or virtual bottleneck).
4   Operations involving flows where no bottlenecks exist are likewise controlled by orders obtained from the market.

The following consequences emerge:

1   Maximum productive output is ensured by optimizing the bottleneck schedule in relation to clients' orders.
2   The reference sequence is provided by the sequence of clients' orders, but it may also be partially modified according to operational problems.

Total Industrial Engineering

TIE is an integrated approach to production engineering, whereby continuous improvement of production processes is sought by involving the entire work force and using specific techniques. Unlike approaches derived from the classical work-study method, TIE possesses the following characteristics:

1   It is oriented toward the efficiency of a whole system instead of efficiency in individuals.
2   It requires participation by all employees, instead of by a privileged few, in examining and implementing measures intended to improve the organization of production and production cycles.

3   It is based on knowledge and continuous use of industrial engineering (IE) techniques (both basic techniques and advanced techniques such as the SEDAC system) by everyone.
4   It tends to motivate employees through activities for improving the organization of production, especially by means of small autonomous groups.

A fuller comprehension of TIE operational aspects can be gained through closer examination of certain significant elements. Employee involvement requires creation of multi-hierarchical working groups. Their composition should be based upon the organizational structure of small improvement groups or of SEDAC (Chapter 6). Analysis and improvement encompass every aspect of production, such as structure of work (personnel, machinery and procedures), work methods, layout, technological processes and production cycles. In particular, these groups pursue waste prevention objectives (in regard to set-up time, for example). The techniques to be used include methods of Taylorist origin, as well as more specific methods oriented toward a process of diagnosis and improvement. These include the following:

- The seven tools
- The seven new tools
- Window Analysis
- Cause-and-Effect Diagram with Addition of Cards (CEDAC)
- On Error Training (OET)
- Window Development (WD)
- Human Error Analysis (HEA)
- Skill analysis
- Day to Day Management (DDM)
- VCS

All of the work analysis techniques of the Taylorist school are extensively used in TIE, although there is a major difference in approach. These techniques are used by operating personnel specifically to improve their own work and to prevent waste, instead of being used to increase the pace of work. Hence, videotapes prepared by the workers themselves are often used to facilitate analysis of their own activities.

Total Productive Maintenance

The TPM approach emerged from Japanese manufacturing industry but is now spreading fast in the West. Examples of results obtained so far in Western factories are the following:

Accidental stoppages per month	From 1,000 to 20
Efficiency of systems	+50%
Quality defects	From 1% to 0.1%
Customers' claims	From 100 to 25
Maintenance costs	−30%
Required inventories	−50%
Value added per employee	+50%
Accidents	None

TPM is consistent with the general objectives of Lean Production and also with specific JIT operational objectives. Its synergy with JIT is highlighted by the following definition: systems and machines must ensure maximum reliability of processes to avoid the need for safety inventories and to obtain efficient, smooth flows. For maintenance to be effective, it must be performed continuously and promptly. TPM meets this need.

The operational links between JIT (in reference to the Toyota Production System) and TPM are clearly shown in Figure 5.3. The six types of loss identified on the right side of the figure are the points of concentration for TPM known as the six big losses. These losses include:

1   Shutdowns resulting from unexpected damage (breakdowns)
2   Set-up and adjustment time
3   Unused time and brief shutdowns
4   Speed below specified levels
5   Losses on account of defects
6   Production losses during starting procedures

The first two losses are caused by stoppages, the next two pertain to speed, and the final two are caused by defects (quality). "Total" efficiency of systems can be improved by eliminating these losses. The Japanese employ an overall equipment effectiveness index, which can be defined in the following form:

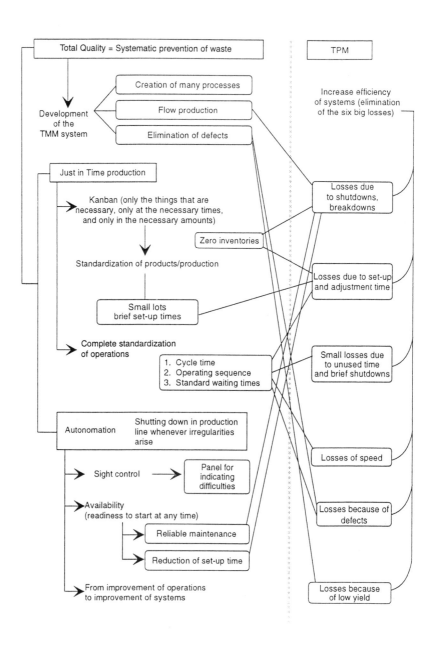

Figure 5.3   *Total productive maintenance in a TMM environment.*

OEE = Level of availability of system × Efficiency × Percentage of acceptable products

To be eligible for the TPM Prize, a factory cannot score lower on this index than 85%. Hence, the six big losses should not surpass 15% of installed time (in other words, total theoretical plant availability). This objective can be pursued by means of the following secondary reference objectives:

1   Stoppages: downtime exceeding 10 minutes for each unit (or system) should occur no more than once per month.
2   Set-up and adjustment time: set-up and adjustment procedures should require no more than 10 minutes.
3   Brief shutdowns and minor losses: these situations should not exceed 10 minutes, and they should not occur more than three times per month.
4   Speed: full speed should be attained for 115% or more of the technical cycle length.
5   Defects in processes: the percentage of defects for each process (including repeat work) should be less than 0.1 percent.
6   Yield: start up yield should allow 99% or more of lot size.

The five basic activities for achieving TPM are to:

1   Improve the efficiency of all machine components
2   Introduce autonomous maintenance
3   Have the maintenance department define a maintenance programme
4   Train maintenance personnel
5   Create a situation of reliability and maintainability right from the moment when equipment is designed

Although these five points provide a concept of the organizational aspects of TPM, it should be remembered that TPM also includes significant technical components, such as operational use of Weibull curves. It should also be observed that, from a technical standpoint, there is significant overlapping between TPM and Statistical Process Control (SPC), especially in regard to managing and improving process capability. In terms of human resources, TPM requires changes in the structuring of work and tasks, in contrast to TIE, which merely produces a direct impact with respect to involvement. Indeed, autonomous maintenance even calls for performance of maintenance tasks by operating personnel. Maintenance activities entrusted to operating personnel are developed gradually, until contact with the maintenance department is necessary only in terms of requests for special procedures, consulting services, support and scheduling.

To summarize, TPM accomplishes "productive maintenance" through involvement of all employees in participating company units (design, production, maintenance, etc.). Specifically, the following measures are carried out:

- The overall efficiency of systems and machinery is perfected through prevention of waste and losses caused by machines (the six big losses)
- The reliability of systems is increased to improve product quality and machine productivity
- Economical systems and plant are developed and controlled throughout their useful life
- All personnel, from top management to workers, are mobilized
- The traditional separation of activities between production personnel and maintenance personnel is removed
- Operating personnel are thoroughly involved and trained to use and maintain systems and machinery
- Workers are motivated through autonomous maintenance activities, which can also be carried out in small groups

TOTAL LOGISTIC STRATEGY

A supply chain (Figure 5.4) is made up of a series of companies and activities, all of which contribute to the production and delivery to the final consumer of a product. The behaviour of each link in a supply chain is influenced by the links preceding and following it. The signals reaching each link tend to be weak because they arise from interpretations of present trends. Because of the present communications systems between the various links, supply chains often are not configured as a

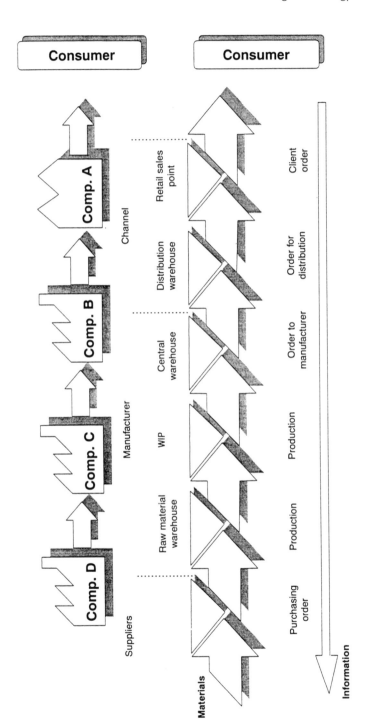

Figure 5.4 Company – supply chain.

rational system. The various links are not transparent to each other and therefore do not help the flow of information and materials. Very often the chain looks like a series of sub-units separated by formalities and bureaucratic delays.

The same tendency is often found within a single company, where company functions, procedures and red tape all contribute to slowing down, filtering and even distorting the information flow. In such a situation small variations in demand are counter-balanced by cyclical oscillations that affect the whole supply chain, rendering it extremely vulnerable. At the origin of these oscillations there are the lack of transparency and the procedures used by the planning systems. Companies at one end of a chain interpret signals coming from companies at the other end of it, such as reductions in stocks, as actual increases in demand. As a result they make wrong decisions. The amplifying effect of demand variations grows the further along the chain it goes. The greater the number of links there are in the chain, the greater the effect becomes. This phenomenon is known as the Forrester effect, after the name of the researcher who put forward the theory at the beginning of the 1960s.

The traditional supply chain is generally so vulnerable because it has the following characteristics:

- Long production and distribution Lead Times
- Stocks distributed at various independent points
- Fragmented information and control flows
- Individual strategies often in conflict, with attempts at "sub-optimizations" rather than the optimization of the whole chain
- Many actors, each of whom have specific requirements

As is clear from this description, no single organization controls the whole business chain and the success of each single company is conditioned by the performance of the whole chain.

A company that wants to be successful, therefore, must evaluate the whole chain to find its own role and the best position for itself. It will thus be able to improve real control, ensure success for the whole chain and obtain the maximum competitive advantage from it. The objective of supply chain management is to plan the whole flow of materials from the suppliers to the final consumers in such a way as to limit the resources necessary and offer the level of service required by each specific market sector. Activities and stocks must be planned and controlled as though they were a single, integrated entity. The companies involved must establish reciprocally advantageous relations that will enable the chain to operate more fluidly and at lower costs. The chain will be efficient if the service needs of the final customers are identified precisely and if stocks are positioned correctly along its length. Lastly, chain efficiency will also be achieved if the right policies and procedures are applied to manage it as a single entity. Modern technology is a great contribution to current developments, thanks to integrated information and control systems, automatic data banks, real time communications and to flexible production.

The objectives to achieve are: a single flow of materials within the supply chain; minimum investments in stocks; maximum flexibility to give more choice and enhance product value for the final consumer; competitive advantage shared by the whole chain; and, lastly, a guarantee of quality at all levels. Integrating the supply chain means strengthening supplier/customer relations, creating barriers against new competitors thanks to the investments made in information and other technologies, making the traditional supply chains uncompetitive and launching products on the market more rapidly.

However, to achieve all these benefits, attitudes towards the traditional supply chain must be changed. In particular the suppliers and the customers (who are the links in the chain) must negotiate in cooperative terms. They must have the same knowledge of the costs that are generated along the chain, pursue a high level of integration within each participating organization and improve communications.

COMAKERSHIP

The policies for developing supplier–client relations are today universally characterized by the following:

• Establishing long-term, stable relationships

- Limiting the number of active suppliers
- Not changing suppliers frequently
- Establishing a global qualification system
- Rating suppliers based on total cost rather than price
- Cooperating with suppliers to make their processes more reliable and less expensive

Cultural changes do not take place by leaps but by small consecutive increments. The process must be planned and guided in a responsible fashion, according to a coherent dynamic model. A model for viewing the evolution of supplier relationships in global terms (from supplier selection to organization) is described here in three levels of development.

Conventional approach
- Prices as a priority
- An adversarial approach to and relationship with conflicting interests, based on strength
- Supplier selection and rating based on price and reliability (deliveries, quality) and always applied to supplier's output
- Entry inspection (100%), managed by acceptable quality level (AQL) and statistical sampling
- Formal certification
- Supplier control by inspection

Outlook: "Suppliers are stores where one shops for the best price."

1st development level (Quality improvement)
- Quality as a priority
- Establishment of long-term relationships
- Experiments with Comakership (pilot projects with some suppliers)
- Reduced number of suppliers
- Supplier rating based on Total Quality cost
- Setting up of self-certification
- Acquisition of systems rather than components (under the guidance of project designers)
- Setting up of JIT supplies

Outlook: "Creating quality together with suppliers."

2nd development level (Operational integration)
- Controlling supplier processes and total processes
- Supplier selection and rating based on supplier's process capabilities
- Widening Comakership (operational integration)
- Some joint R&D investments
- Setting up of product and process codesign
- Joint improvement plans with suppliers
- Widespread self-certification
- Widespread JIT and setting up of synchronized supplies
- Market feedback directly to suppliers
- Connected Quality Assurance systems

Outlook: "The production process begins in the supplier's departments."

3rd development level (Strategic integration)
- Joint business process control
- Global supplier rating (as well as technological and strategic)
- Widespread product and process codesign (with quality function deployment)
- Business partnership with some important suppliers
- Market feedback in "real time" with direct field diagnoses
- Widespread synchronized supplies
- Agreements at the highest level concerning strategies and policies
- Total Quality Assurance systems (integrated)

Outlook: "Doing business together."

From the perspective of operational relations in Western companies, three reference classes or levels are taking shape as a function of the degree to which the Comakership relationship has evolved:

- Class III: The conventional supplier
- Class II: The associated supplier (operational Comakership)
- Class I: The partner supplier (global Comakership/business partnership)

Given that most suppliers start out in Class III, the issue is determining which of them to move into Class II and, eventually, Class I. Of course, even in advanced situations, there always exist suppliers in Classes III and II. This is a function of a company's ability to influence its supplier pool, by reason of opportunity (which might also be economic) linked to an (ABC) classes analysis (or to Kraljic matrix). The following sections summarize the types of relationship that may be established with suppliers as a function of the class to which they belong.

Class III: The Conventional Supplier

Negotiations based on minimal qualitative specifications and on price. This means that, concerning supplies from suppliers of this class (either by choice or by need, as we shall see in the chapter pertaining to purchase marketing), the client company finds all the suppliers available in the marketplace, on the basis of the minimum acceptable qualitative specifications, and then chooses the ones able to guarantee the lowest price. This is done by managing two or three suppliers at the same time, in order both to have alternative sources and to create a price competition.

Supplies based on single, short-term orders. No guarantee is provided to the supplier concerning future orders, which are all to be "earned" based on the prices quoted at the next request. It makes no sense, except as a means for exercising psychological pressure, to inform the supplier about expected future needs.

Regular testing of supplies ("acceptance"). Such supplies, whose only Quality Assurance is in the signing of a contract providing for possible penalties (but not always), must, of course, be 100% checked before they are accepted and forwarded. The possibility of testing only a statistical sample, or even of allowing free pass, are both risks that the client company can take unilaterally based on historical data or on the low level of importance of the component involved.

The need to prevent stock shortages. A situation in which a supplier has been rated only on its output (price, service and quality provided) presupposes some risks due to not knowing whether its performance can be guaranteed over time. For example, it might be able to provide the quality required only through considerable production waste or provide proper service only through large inventory. This involves a risk for the client company that does not exist when the supplier's processes are "at risk" with regard to quality guarantees and the ability to respond to changes of plan. For this reason the client company finds it necessary to protect itself by keeping reserve stocks of such materials to be sure it will not have shortages.

The adversarial game connected to a Class III situation could reach extreme manifestations, such as a client taking advantage of a coupler's difficult times to obtain favourable prices or a supplier taking advantage of a client's production crunch times to palm off unsold stock, even at a high price. Given that the relationship is anything but one of mutual trust, the need to protect the client company with systems (inspection and security) is obvious.

Class II: The Associated Supplier (Operational Comakership)

This is an intermediate level between the conventional supplier and the true comaker. Comakership in this context is limited to operational activities. Such a relationship is characterized by the following:

A long-term relationship, which is periodically reviewed. This type of supplier, once it has become a regular supplier and has the necessary features to remain such, is not set in competition against its competitors at every purchase but benefits from a middle- to long-term policy. The conditions for such a relationship are redefined each year (sometimes they are simply updated) on the basis of purchase marketing research. When an "interesting" alternative supplier is found, the procedure for a substitution is not immediately implemented; rather, an attempt is made to "rehabilitate" the associated supplier, even helping it to reach the level of its competition.

The possibility of price fluctuations on the basis of agreed-on criteria. The price of supplies is protected by autonomic fluctuation mechanisms. The criteria might involve linking prices to simple indexes showing the trends in raw materials and labour costs or else referring to the average prices in that supply market. The latter approach is possible only when the client company is equipped with sufficient capability for analyzing the market (purchase marketing) and when sufficient trust exists between the two parties. In any case, some degree of fluctuation is expected without activating updates (for example, 11% of the average market price).

Guaranteed and self-certified quality, on the basis of agreed-on criteria. An associated supplier knows the purpose of its supplies and therefore the functions to be exercised by its products. In order to become "associated", the supplier would also have undergone a process capability evaluation by the client to ascertain that it has the capability and information it needs to avoid providing products that are not up to standard. If products that do not conform are delivered twice in a row, for example, serious doubts would arise about its capability or good faith. Such an event could justify its being cancelled as a supplier for not keeping its end of the bargain. Self-certification, though a signed acknowledgement of responsibility, could constitute the first necessary step in establishing this type of relationship, but with the aim to a self-certification "guarantee" signed once and for all, not *ad hoc* documents, which, in the end, are simply expensive and bureaucratic.

Comprehensive responsibility for the supplies furnished. In the context of the relationship described in the above item, the supplier is invested with the entire responsibility for the consequences of any nonconformity of the product sold (product liability). Under most applicable laws, the client company maintains that responsibility toward the final customer or user. In any case, the laws of both the USA and the European Community promote such a principle by requiring traceability of components.

No acceptance testing ("free pass"). Suppliers that have proved their reliability concerning quality and are fully responsible for it will benefit from a free pass arrangement, thus eliminating entry testing (acceptance). The free pass will generate economic savings for the client as well, in terms of elimination of inspection, reduction of stocks and reduction of Lead Time (work-in-process) and of the planning horizon. It is normal for Japanese companies (and not infrequent for Western companies) that reach free pass with a supplier to return a premium equal to (or half) the amount saved by the client company by eliminating the cost of testing.

Direct supplies to departments in a pull flow, without reserve stocks. Once the need for testing is eliminated, along with the need for reserve stocks awaiting inspection, a company using a JIT organization can direct supplies straight to the production departments. This involves considerable modifications to the company's logistic system, but the advantages are enormous: the supplier feeds the production workplace directly, without intermediate storing, testing, pick-up and supply handling, or intermediate transportation.

Frequent supplies, in small lots, on an open-order basis. The system becomes extraordinarily economical when the two preceding items can be put into effect. At that point implementation of JIT logistics becomes possible, which involves receiving small lots of supplies with a much greater frequency than previously. It is quite normal to go from monthly supply lots to daily deliveries, or even more frequent ones (in some Japanese companies, as often as every ten minutes).

Systematic improvement in the quality and price of the products supplied. This is particularly important: if a supplier company "marries" a client company, it must become an active component in the client's strategies. A company that makes associates of its suppliers is certainly a company aiming for a Total Quality logic and, consequently, relying on programmes for continual improvement. The supplier cannot exempt itself from this excellence-seeking strategy; it must contribute its part by guaranteeing continued improvements. This factor may be set forth among the contractual terms, where a supplier might, for example, undertake to reduce real prices by 3% a year, while improving quality by 30%.

Consulting and training suppliers. It is in the best interest of the client company that the supplier should continue to increase its organizational and technical capacity. The client will therefore invest in actions and resources aimed at the supplier's organizational development. The client's contribution, at a minimum, will include conveying information necessary for fully integrating the supplier within its operational logic. On a greater level, the client may provide full consulting support (from qualitative problems to organizational and managerial problems). The smaller the supplier and the more integral it is to the client's structure, the more the client will benefit from offering the second type of support.

Class I: The Partner Supplier (Global Comakership)

This case concerns a global Comakership, which takes on the characteristics of a business partnership. The operational relationship is similar to that of Class II. Its other specific characteristics include the following:

Cooperation in designing new products and technologies. This type of supplier is integrated in the operations of the client company and also contributes to the development of their joint business (the supplier lives for the client's business, and the client lives for the supplier's ability to make it possible). Almost always, most of the components of a client company's design are based on and contain the supplier's technology. Under the less evolved circumstances, when the client's designers develop a product, they also establish in advance which technologies the supplier will use and in fact require a predetermined component from the supplier. Quite apart from the fact that these designers cannot know all of a supplier's technologies, consider how many opportunities could be lost, in terms of both cost and function, if the real experts in these technologies are not involved.

Involving suppliers in the design as codesigners constitutes a definite competitive advantage; in Western companies, however, such a cultural evolution is not easily attained. Such an integration, focused on the product, can be carried out only with a limited number of suppliers, after careful analysis and evaluation. The administrations of each party must often reach strategic agreements. The most commonly practised and recommended approach involves the development within the client company of the capability to design just the overall "system" for a product within the client company, requiring the suppliers to develop the components. This is an "engineering company" logic. Everything said thus far concerning product design applies as well to other aspects of business that the companies share – strategies, systems, resources, and so on, as in a business partnership.

Joint investments in R&D and in technological achievement. This item is a direct consequence of the preceding one.

Constant exchange of information concerning processes and products. Immediate feedback from the client company's market directly to the supplier allows the parties to make quick global estimates and promptly introduce the required changes or improvements. It makes available information and ideas that are very useful to both parties. This is a matter of carrying out the world class logic of an "open" company (both upstream and downstream).

Figure 5.5 summarizes the criteria and reference contents to be used in relations with suppliers at the three proposed operational levels (conventional, associated and partner suppliers). The elements analyzed in relation to the three levels are:

• Quality management
• Logistical aspects
• Involvement in product and technology development
• Supplier rating

CONCURRENT ENGINEERING

Following a period in which the focus was on manufacturing, the process of designing and industrialization of new products is coming to the forefront of companies' strategic development. It is this process that determines and conditions much of the quality factor (a good deal of the negative quality, all reliability and all positive quality), all time to market, almost all productive flexibility (technologies, components, production cycles) and lastly, most of the cost of the product.

   Developments in this process towards a new type of rationale have led to the configuration of new operative procedures called Forward/Simultaneous/Concurrent Engineering (these three terms are virtually synonymous). This subject really requires considerable technical detail but I intend here to deal only with the organizational aspects and to give a list of the methodologies

Supplier level	Subsystems			
	Quality	Logistics	Product and technology development	Supplier rating
Class III: Conventional	• The supplier is responsible to furnish in accordance with quality specifications • The client makes incoming inspections and source inspections	• Suppliers "order by phone" with specific delivery times • Need for safety stocks	• Product and component characteristics designed solely by client • First sample verification	• Price • Quality performance (output) • Logistic performance (output) • Inspection of supplier's quality control system and certification • Quality assurance manuals
Class II: associated	• Self-certification (supplier) • Free pass (client) • Quality improvement programme (supplier–client)	• Long-term contracts • JIT/synchronized deliveries directly to production dept. (no stocks) • Continuous reduction of stock and Lead Times (together)	• Technical requirements of components and technology defined with supplier • Supplier consulted in advance	• Total cost evaluations • Audit of supplier's system • Audit of supplier's processes (process capabilities and management)
Class I: partner	• The supplier is responsible for the conformity of components to final customer satisfaction • Continuous improvement together • Codesign of Quality requirements	• Supplier integrated in the client's logistic process (same documents, same operative system) • Shared information and planning system (electronic data interchange network)	• Supplier involved in the development process, starting from product concept • Supplier involved in product planning process • Supplier proactive	• Global evaluations (quality, logistics, process capability, management system) • Evaluation of supplier's strategies

Figure 5.5 Supplier–client operational model.

employed to enable my readers to evaluate and make managerial use of them.

Concurrent Engineering is an approach through which "time to market" and "quality", two fundamental strategic priorities in the present scenario, can be pursued in a precise and effective way, while at the same time, of course, maintaining the necessary product cost reduction trend. The "quality" objective includes two dimensions:

1 The capacity to design products with a high customer-satisfaction potential (conformity to purpose)
2 The capacity to reduce drastically the "non-quality" costs due to:
   - Modifications to the product and equipment
   - Problems during production
   - Customers' problems in use (costs of technical assistance)

Much emphasis is placed on prevention, especially concerning the last point. The prevention concept is promoted in many companies by the slogan "10 ×" ("10 times"), which means the following:

- Eliminating a defect on the customer's premises costs at least 10 times more than it would at the manufacturing level (outside repairs are costly and have negative impacts on product and company images)
- Eliminating a defect at the manufacturing level costs at least 10 times more than it would at the engineering level
- Eliminating a defect at the engineering level costs at least 10 times more than it would at the design level (because plant already constructed has to be modified)

The consequence is that the cost of eliminating a defect is probably 1000 times lower at the design level than at the final customer level. Therefore, a Concurrent Engineering objective is to move these corrections further and further upstream, eventually to the planning and designing level (Figure 5.6).

The "quality" objective is pursued through the combined adoption of organizing, methodological and technical approaches. The organizing and methodological dimension is called Quality Function Deployment (QFD). Through it the development of a new product can be set up correctly right from the beginning. The point of departure, in fact, is the customer's requirements (both expressed and potential). QFD permits the "customer's voice" to be heard in all the phases of product development, right down to the definition of production specifications and the process variables to be supervised, thus reducing to a minimum the need for later modifications. The logic followed by QFD is shown in Figure 5.7.

First, QFD concentrates on the pursuit of customer satisfaction – those identified as positive quality factors. The aspects more closely connected with negative quality, defects and the cost of non-quality, are pursued more specifically by certain technical and methodological approaches. These include:

- Design of Experiments (DOE)
- Robust Design (RD)
- Reliability techniques
- Design for Manufacturing and Assembling (DFMA)
- Design Review (DR)
- Value Analysis (VA)
- Value Engineering (VE)

A brief description of each of these approaches follows:

Design of Experiments (DOE). This consists of the application of advanced statistical techniques to optimize experimentation, reducing the number of tests to a minimum and evaluating the influence of the various parameters of the product and the process on the product's characteristic performances.

Robust Design (RD). This is a design approach aimed at determining the most stable and therefore most robust configuration of a system. A system is considered robust when, besides satisfying the requirements for which it was designed, it does not amplify the imperfections inherent in the design and construction processes of the system, but attenuates them at the performance response level.

Reliability techniques. These are aimed at foreseeing and preventing possible breakdown modes of a product or a process and eliminating their causes at the design level.

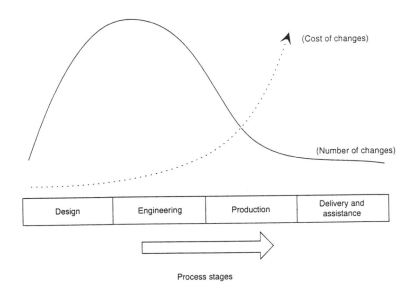

Figure 5.6   *Moving corrections upstream (target configuration).*

Design for Manufacturing and Assembling (DFMA). These are procedures for studying the single components of a product so as to:

• Reduce the number of components in a product
• Reduce the time and difficulties involved in production and assembling
• Standardize components for product families

Design Review (DR), Value Analysis (VA) and Value Engineering (VE). The objective of these methodologies is to review a project in critical terms, evaluating its degree of conformity with its purpose and the value/cost ratio of the functions, components, equipment and operations. The time objective of Concurrent Engineering is pursued through a combined action that includes not only the reduction of time lost over quality problems (as just described), but also a review of the whole new product development process and a reduction of the time necessary for each separate stage of the process.

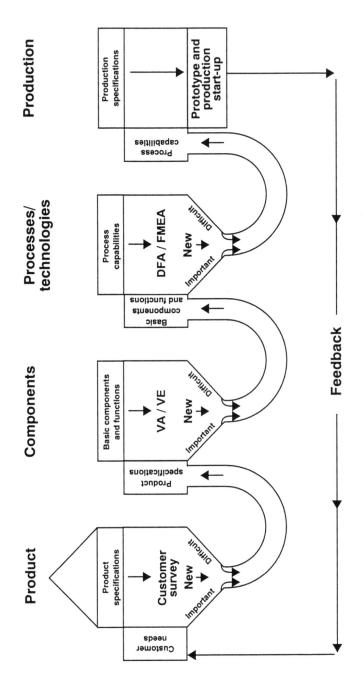

Figure 5.7   *The process developed through QFD: The "voice of the customer" enters the company.*

Reorganizational Factors are Dealt with by BPR.

They concern both the sequence of the stages and the organizational methods for putting them into action. The objective of Concurrent Engineering is to reduce the need to work in sequence, to put forward the stages previously executed downstream or to execute them in parallel. In fact the very name Concurrent Engineering refers to the objective of engineering a product at the same time as its design is developed. This is both to reduce the times involved and to interact with the designers over potential manufacturing problems that can be foreseen right from the start by the engineers and manufacturers.

Concurrent Engineering deals with organizational methods by abandoning all functional and Taylorist ideas, with their transmittal of instructions from one group to another, to the advantage of greater integration along the process and the frequent use of product teams. This method guarantees that the concerns (or rather points of view) of the various functions are constantly represented and included in the project development process. It also eliminates those exhausting ping-pong exchanges between functions, the only results of which are to elongate designing times and raise costs, without ensuring that the result of all the work is that exact product that responds precisely to the openings indicated by marketing or generated by R&D. This change is conceptually illustrated in Figure 5.8.

The product team can be made up by temporary aggregations of people from the various functions concerned, who dedicate their whole time to the development of a new product. They are put physically together in one place, a working method much used by the Japanese, who call it designing by "rooms" (product room). Another system is to create a product team made up of full-time or part-time work groups, the mix being variable in time and managed by a product-chief. In both cases the group is responsible for the development and improvement in time of the product. The group follows various products at different points in their life cycle (e.g. successive generations, one already mature, another at the development stage). The head of the group is the product leader.

Management by Processes is the different managerial dimension necessary for improvement. It guarantees that the development process of new products is managed through the use of

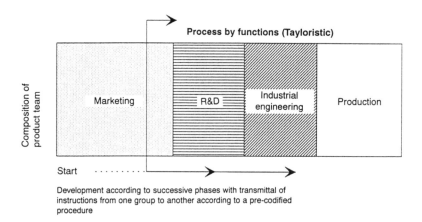

Development according to successive phases with transmittal of
instructions from one group to another according to a pre-codified
procedure

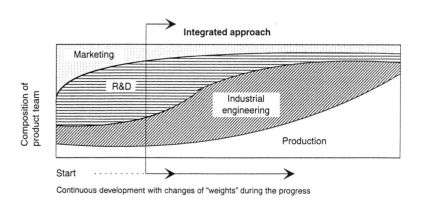

Continuous development with changes of "weights" during the progress

Figure 5.8   *New product development: Tayloristic vs integrated approach.*

managerial indicators ensuring a continuous pressure on time reduction at every stage and on output quality improvement. The methodology used is described in Chapter 7. The objective "continuous reduction of costs" in new product development is pursued, of course, at the same time as the objectives "quality" and "time", and is already included in most of the procedures cited for the other two objectives. The approaches and procedures most suitable for reducing costs are DOE, DFMA, the reliability techniques and VA. However, there are certain strategic aspects that influence development in new products, based on higher rationales than Forward Engineering. They are the consequences of company strategic policies with a more general impact. Among others I will cite codesign, carry over and the mushroom concept. Codesign refers to the decision to involve suppliers of parts or components in the design phase of new products.

Carry over means limiting as much as possible any changes in components which have no influence on the image of a product, while maintaining components of proven reliability. This reduces the risk of defects (greater reliability) and guarantees lower costs. In general this approach is combined with a shortening of the life cycle of a product. This means fewer innovations on new products but more frequent innovations on the market.

In the mushroom concept, there is little diversification in the product structure at the first levels but it explodes laterally at the last levels. The structure of the product and the processes (technological layout) look like a mushroom, as shown in Figure 5.9. The result is that product structures are more flexible, are more easily personalized and have lower total costs because of the drastic reduction in the number of component parts.

To sum up, Concurrent Engineering may be seen as an approach based on a new managerial and organizational dimension, operating in the context of new strategic priorities, with the addition of new procedures and specific methodologies. I think it may be helpful to emphasize the fact that the approach dealt with here is determined much more by organizational and cultural changes than by specific procedures, which can even become an extra onus if they are not used in synergy with each other, thanks to adequate organization and management.

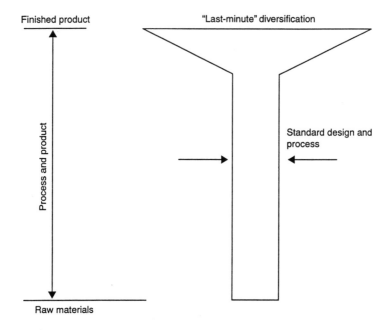

Figure 5.9   *Mushroom concept product structure.*

6
Operational Management

In Chapter 3 we saw how priority objectives are to be identified and planned. I also evaluated the types of objective and made particular reference to the methods for tackling them. Two categories of objectives were identified: those to be pursued through organizational revisions and those to be dealt with by the line management. The Business Process Reengineering (BPR) approach was proposed for reorganizing objectives (Chapter 4), while the Effective Management approach was suggested for in-line management.

In this chapter I will deal in depth with this special management system. I will illustrate methods providing effectiveness in the operative management of Breakthrough objectives – the process of "transforming objectives into results". I will propose an operative organization based on approaches and tools that are a simplified combination of worldwide best practices. The philosophy behind this formula comes from the Japanese Management by Policy, the pragmatism from American practice and the characteristic approach from successful entrepreneurs working in small and medium-sized companies in Europe. The whole approach is governed by visual management tools developed by Ryuji Fukuda (who was awarded the Deming Prize for these methods) and by Galgano & Associates. The method is now in use by dozens of companies, both large and small, including most of those quoted as examples in Chapter 1.*

---

* The subject is dealt with more exhaustively in G. Merli, *Breakthrough Management*, John Wiley & Sons, Chichester 1995, of which this chapter is a synthesis.

THE EFFECTIVE MANAGEMENT PROCESS

The Effective Management process requires the following abilities:

- Identifying priority operating objectives
- Assigning the right responsibilities
- Identifying the most appropriate operating indicators and targets
- Managing priorities "in real time" (day by day)
- "Visual supervision" of the indicators of the priority objectives
- Detecting the current bottlenecks blocking the priority objectives
- Dealing effectively with the bottlenecks

The requirements bring to life the basic principle of Breakthrough management ("the entrepreneur's dream"), which is "the main task of a manager at each level is to work every day on the priority business objectives, and to concentrate on removing the bottlenecks in the process on which their achievement depends". Let us now see how it is possible to satisfy these "seven requirements of Breakthrough management" through an operating process.

The problem of identifying priority objectives has been dealt with in Chapter 4, while the criteria for Effective Management were discussed in Chapter 3. It now remains to describe the operating process by which the other requirements can be met. The overall design of the process is illustrated in Figure 6.1. It makes ample use of the visual management tools of the Ryuji Fukuda Structure for Enhancing Daily Activities through Creativity (SEDAC) system. This set of tools supports all Breakthrough management needs, starting from the second requirement listed above, but is particularly effective compared with current methodologies from the fourth requirement onwards (the ability to manage priorities in "real time").

The management approach proposed is based exclusively on operating indicators as opposed to traditional management

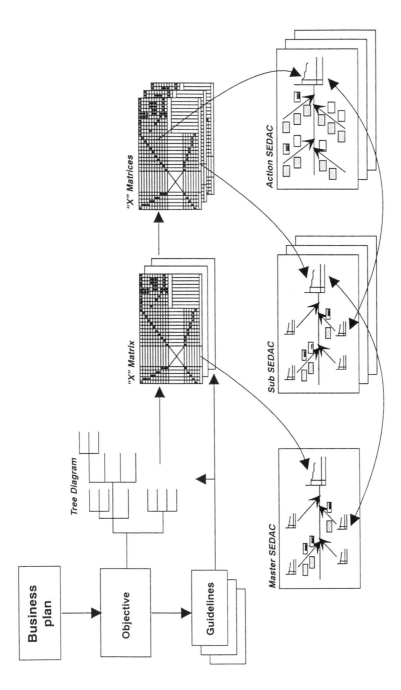

Figure 6.1   *The Effective Management process.*

reporting focused on results. Its operating process is based on the use of four sequential phases which make up the Breakthrough management cycle. The four phases are as follows:

1 Planning and programming
2 Organizing management
3 Operating
4 Monitoring and management

PLANNING AND PROGRAMMING

This phase concerns the identification and planning of the actions required to pursue the Breakthrough objectives chosen for special management by the line. It generally concerns objectives for the improvement of operating performance. The process which turns a priority objective into a coherent operating plan of synergic actions is normally called Policy Deployment (or Hoshin Planning). The term "Policy", borrowed from Management by Policy, picks up and highlights all the various elements which should be taken into account in launching actions to achieve an objective. These elements consist of:

• Type of objective (the improvement "direction")
• Indicators and numerical targets
• Reference guidelines
• Constraints and assumptions

These are indispensable to Breakthrough management taken in its widest entrepreneurial sense as described in the Chapter 3. The prime requirement is for the objective to be clearly identified and defined in terms of satisfactory results (indicators and targets). The second requirement is for the objective to be coherent with the other short- and medium-term objectives (this is ensured by the guidelines or by the policies themselves). The third requirement is for it to be compatible with the resources available and with the economic parameters of the budget, and that it should not prejudice other areas of performance (these are protected by the "constraints and assumptions").

Coming now to the meaning of "Deployment", which is more or less synonymous with breakdown or explosion. Policy Deployment is a methodological process which permits the "cascade" breakdown of a policy or an objective into:

- Improvement areas
- Operating indicators and targets
- Responsibilities
- Projects/actions
- Resources
- Time scale

The action plan, which has been derived from Policy Deployment, must take in everything that is necessary and sufficient to obtain the desired result. Deployment must be done "by priority", in the sense that at each level only the priority factors are broken down and included in the special management arrangements.

The choice of priorities at each deployment level should be tailor-made and not simply be a Pareto approach based on the relative importance of the factors considered. The criteria for choosing priorities should not simply be their arithmetic impact on the objective (their relative "weight"), but should be the product of "weight × ease of achievement". This means that we shall seek out the best combination between the weight of the factor and the estimated likelihood of getting results out of it. In Total Quality jargon, we are looking for the best combination of $B \times Q$ (where B stands for "level of impact on the business" and Q = Quality for "existing improvement margins"). By "tailor-made", on the other hand, we mean that once the priorities have been identified, we replan the numerical target to be assigned to them. If, for example, the deployment process has initially identified the need to improve five indicators by 5–7% and three by 15–20%, once the priorities have been decided the targets will be redefined raising the objectives for the priority factors and probably reducing the others. This makes use of the concept that "effectiveness equals concentrating on priorities". Priorities are identified so that special management can be applied to them in order to reach a high level of effectiveness. We shall probably not be able to supervise the other factors with the same attention and effectiveness. This means that we must extract the maximum effectiveness from special management and obtain the most significant results possible.

"Tailor-made" can however, have an even broader meaning. This is in the unfortunate case where deployment does not highlight any priority factors or objectives (a "flat Pareto" where a large number of factors/objectives appear all with the same order of importance or difficulty). In this case, to arrive at a focused entrepreneurial management approach we must "force" the situation and make ourselves choose some priorities. In this process some objectives will be emphasized so as to create the more focused situation required for Breakthrough management. It is perhaps worth recalling that the capacity to "Manage by Priorities" is a basic requirement of entrepreneurial management which is conceptually the opposite of the "optimizing" management capacity, based on supervising large numbers of objectives and indicators. It must also be remembered that "entrepreneurial management" is synonymous with the capacities of the human being, whereas "optimizing management" is synonymous with management through systems and data management capabilities.

Management based on the supervision of two or three factors rather than 10 or 20 is therefore more human and entrepreneurial. In fact it will be easier to achieve improvements of 30% in two to three "manageable" areas than 5–10% in 10 to 20 areas which are only "controllable".

The final principle of Policy Deployment for Breakthrough management is that it should cascade down to the lowest possible levels and identify each elementary action necessary and the individual operating targets. It is very likely that at this level we are talking about foremen, clerical workers and manual workers. At the same time we shall probably not need to involve all of the managers, even at senior levels, since deployment rather than seeking to satisfy hierarchical criteria searches out only those actions and those responsibilities which can genuinely contribute to the achievement of the priority objectives, wherever they may be.

The priority elements identified through the deployment process will be called red objectives, which are generated by business priorities. Staff not directly involved in the management of the "red" objectives of a management cycle are normally used as support staff. They deal with the management of other "green" objectives, derived from "local" priorities which they themselves have identified (also using the "cascade" approach applied to their own area). What is certain is that a "green" objective can never block a "red" objective, even if the person responsible for the green objective has a higher grade than the one responsible for the red objective with which he or she could interfere (with the result or with the use of resources).

This concept can potentially have an even stronger impact and offer an even greater opportunity for improving the management of the business (although it is equally true that it can represent a problem for very functional/hierarchical cultures). The basic management criterion involved is that "in the operations of a business it is the objective that must be in command, not the hierarchy". This means that the management mechanisms must allow for actions where, depending on the skills required, persons of a lower grade may have to manage the contribution of people of a higher grade than themselves. Without entering into its possible organizational implications (to be seen as opportunities rather than a necessity), let us simply accept this principle for the purposes of special management and therefore as an exception. We shall certainly be more effective.

Returning to the Policy Deployment process, it must be stressed that it is not carried out by programmes, or by the managers themselves as a desk exercise. It requires each level of deployment to be agreed with the persons concerned. In practice three hierarchical levels are normally involved for each level of deployment (levels in terms of objectives, not of position). It should moreover be noted that today in a "lean" company, even if it is very large, there should not be more than three levels in its organization concerned with operations. The involvement of three levels is a direct consequence of the planning procedure. Each level is involved with the level above in receiving inputs regarding policies and targets. It is then involved with the level below for the same reasons, and returns to the higher level in order to readjust the first hypothesis (in Management by Policy this approach is called "catch ball").

The whole is a reiterative process which can go through a number of cycles. The result of this procedure will be a plan accepted at all levels, including agreement on targets, the means for pursuing them, and particularly on the indicators to be managed. It should be observed that the contents of a plan developed by the use of Policy Deployment are also different from the contents of a traditional budget. In fact it is not so much a deployment of objectives as a deployment of the actions necessary to achieve the objectives. That is because the objective of an effective plan is not to build a reference for management reporting but to provide line management with the operating indicators and targets which they require to achieve the planned results.

A good deployment will therefore, at each level in the breakdown, take two steps which are fundamental to Breakthrough management:

1   From the general to the particular
2   From the effect to the cause

"From the general to the particular" means that deployment must succeed in identifying all the "therefore" priorities through which the desired overall result can be obtained. "From the effect to the cause" means that to be effective, deployment must at each stage identify the priority causal factors to be tackled in order to obtain the result.

The Japanese call this process upstream control, and the corresponding system as "Management by Process/Cause" instead of "by results". A criticism frequently levelled at our Breakthrough plans by Japanese managers is that they often look very similar to our budgets (sometimes with more detail, sometimes with less). They look more useful for management reporting or control than for operating management, very often simply setting out the deployment of the objectives into sub-objectives in the form of results and subsidiary results expected, rather than the improvements which must be made upstream to the causes. This is another key step: to understand that to be effective in improving results, we must above all know how to identify the principal "levers" for obtaining them; that is, the variables in the processes upstream on which the results depend. For example, if the objective is to improve the quality of a product by 50%, the first deployment level (management, not budgetary) must consist of identifying the main cause of defects (e.g. assembly and machining) and not simply the types of defect; the second level must identify the underlying causes (e.g. heat treatment and work cycles); and the third level, causes even further upstream (e.g. the process capabilities of the oven temperature and deficiencies in the work cycle descriptions) (Figure 6.2).

In this way we shall be able to work out a plan which, by setting up a Breakthrough in the oven temperature process capability and in the preparation of the assembly cycles, will make it possible to obtain a corresponding Breakthrough improvement in the quality of the final product. The alternative would have been to rely on a plan broken out into a mass of 50% improvements which when added up might (possibly) have produced a similar improvement in output, but which would have involved a much bigger, more burdensome operation to manage. The management priorities which in this case can already guarantee 80% or more of the final result were identified as "oven temperature process capability" and "number of cycle lines not defined". Breakthrough operating management will therefore focus on these in order to obtain rapid results. It is as if we had identified the "critical path" towards the objective and avoided fragmenting our efforts ineffectively on everything. In reality the example is deliberately over-simplified, since at the lowest level of deployment there are usually more than two priorities (although this can happen when they are bottlenecks). The remaining 10–20% of the result will be picked up through normal local "bottom-up" or "campaign" improvement management, without tight supervision or special management arrangements.

Returning to the Policy Deployment process, it is also useful to think of the time dimension. How long should a Policy Deployment cycle last; that is, the time taken to make a Breakthrough objectives plan? It should take between one week and two months. Why such a wide bracket of time? It is because the time taken (and the validity of the plan) depends on many factors, in particular the level of knowledge of cause-and-effect relationships inside the firm. It is not by accident that the Japanese claim that they are capable of good deployment today because they have invested thirty years of research into cause-and-effect relationships! The time taken will be very short if there is a detailed knowledge of these relationships, and very

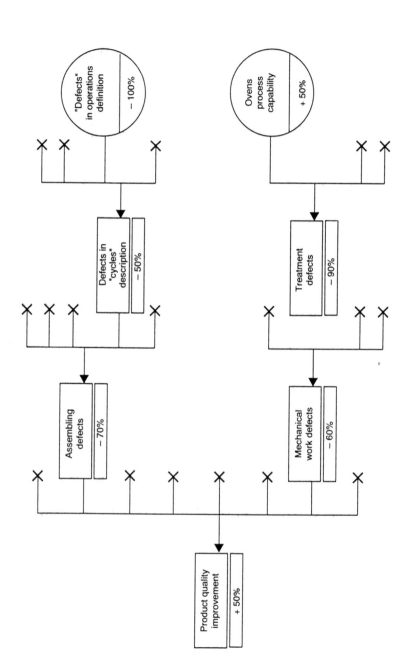

Figure 6.2 An example of deployment by "cause" and "priority".

long if not enough is known, and research and analysis of historical data are necessary. The time will also be very short if almost nothing is known: without abandoning effective planning it will be necessary to use a very different reinteractive or iterative process, and afterwards refine it through a series of more detailed phases.

This first deployment will then simply consist of indicators representing the results that we want to achieve. It is impossible to do anything else if we do not have enough information to identify the "leverage" or causal factors. Deployment will be very fast, only needing qualitative and arithmetical expressions.

This first deployment, although it already aims at achieving some results, will mainly be used to search out the causes, the levers to be used to obtain the results and therefore the indicators for the upstream variables among which we must look for priorities (in this case the "Plan" of Plan, Do, Check, Act (PDCA) will be going on partly at the same time as "Check" and "Act").

SEDAC cascade diagram applications (see below) are very useful in this situation. These are in fact tools designed for the interactive supervision of the phases Plan, Do, Check and Act at the same time, but they are also useful for the phase in which the real causes of a problem or obstacles in the way of an objective are studied. The outcome of this initial research will allow us to move progressively towards a more informed and focused deployment (using better cause-and-effect flows).

Returning to the simplified process methodologies suggested, the best tool for effective deployment is the Tree Diagram, one of the seven management tools developed by the Japanese (the other six are the Affinity Diagram – useful for defining vague objectives, the Relationships Diagram, the Matrix Diagram, the Arrow Diagram, the Matrix-Data Analysis and the Decision Tree). Figure 6.3 illustrates the use of the Tree Diagram.

Its use in the reference framework proposed is shown in Figure 6.4. I suggest that the following criteria should be applied when it is used in Breakthrough management:

- Identify the priorities at each level of deployment, based on data, cause-and-effect analyses, and on "entrepreneurial" decisions (subjective evaluations)

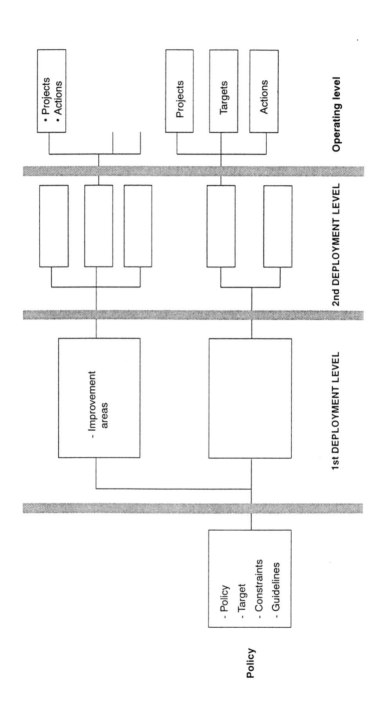

Figure 6.3   *Tree deployment.*

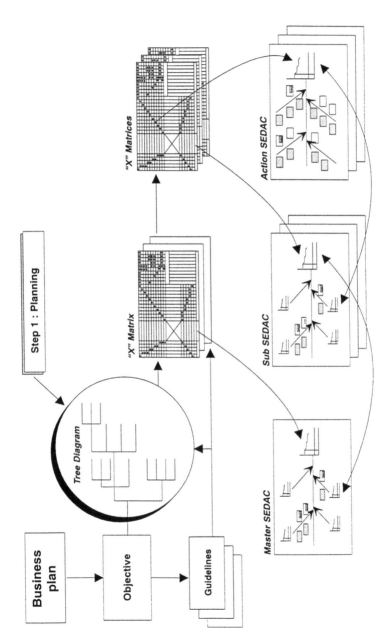

Figure 6.4   *The Effective Management cycle: Planning.*

- Describe them using the most appropriate management indicators (cause/upstream variables)
- On the priority "branches", complete the deployment down to the operating level (projects, operating actions to be launched)
- Interrupt deployment on the non-priority branches
- Obtain consensus at each deployment level (involving the levels above and below)

The results of the planning phase carried out using the Policy Deployment process should therefore be presented in "tree" form. It represents what we want to achieve, and is the starting point for setting up the management arrangements. Figure 6.5 shows the Tree Diagram which will be used as a study case for developing the remaining phases.

ORGANIZING MANAGEMENT

Objectives and Approach

Once we have defined the priorities, the indicators and the targets at each deployment level using the Tree Diagram, we can then move on to the phase of organizing their management. In terms of methodological content this is the most complex phase of the process. It is also the most important phase of special management, since its output defines where it is possible to apply the real time visual management approach which is fundamental to operating effectiveness.

This phase is concerned with Step 2 of Figure 6.6. It can be considered as the bridge between planning and operating. The objective of the organizing management phase is to create an effective link between planning and operating management by:

1. "Mapping out" the organization required to pursue the objective
2. Setting up the visual supervision of the entire operating management process

The instrument recommended for mapping is the Policy/Objective Matrix, usually called the P/O Matrix or the X

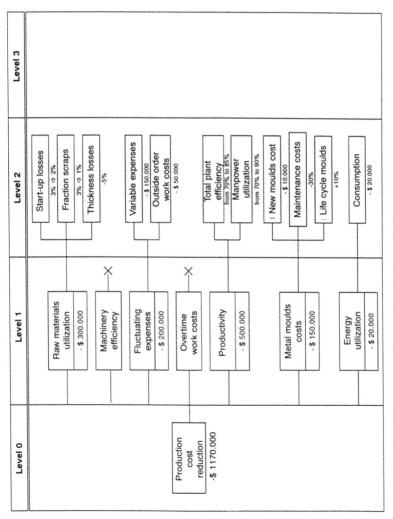

Figure 6.5 *Tree Diagram – study case: Production reduction.*

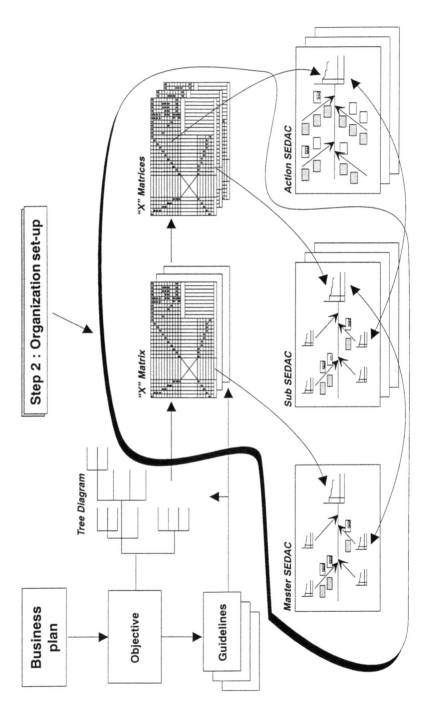

Figure 6.6   The Effective Management cycle: Organization set-up.

Matrix after its shape. The methodology proposed for setting up visual supervision is the SEDAC system and in particular Master and Sub SEDAC.

The X Matrix

The X Matrix contains the following information:

1 A summary of the ways in which it is intended to pursue the objective and in particular the operating targets selected
2 The assignment of responsibilities for the indicator targets
3 The policy guidelines associated with the various projects/ actions
4 The organization planned for pursuing the targets
5 The timetable for the project/actions

The first point covers the horizontal summaries of what has been planned in the Tree Diagrams at each level. This means that there will be a Tree Diagram for each group of homogeneous objectives; that is, for each explosion of a branch of the Tree Diagram and at each level. See the example of a first level X Matrix in Figure 6.7, developed from the example given in Figure 6.5.

From one first level X Matrix there can be three to five second level X Matrices and six to 10, if necessary, at the third level. The number of matrices required depends on the degree of break-down of the Tree Diagram which is their prime source of data. A complete deployment process is therefore summarized in a cascade of X Matrices.

The type of information and data included in the X Matrices will depend on the deployment level to which they refer and the "business maturity" of the firm in terms of Breakthrough management/Management by Policy. For a first level matrix it may be sufficient to include the following data:

• General objective
• Improvement areas
• Indicators
• Targets

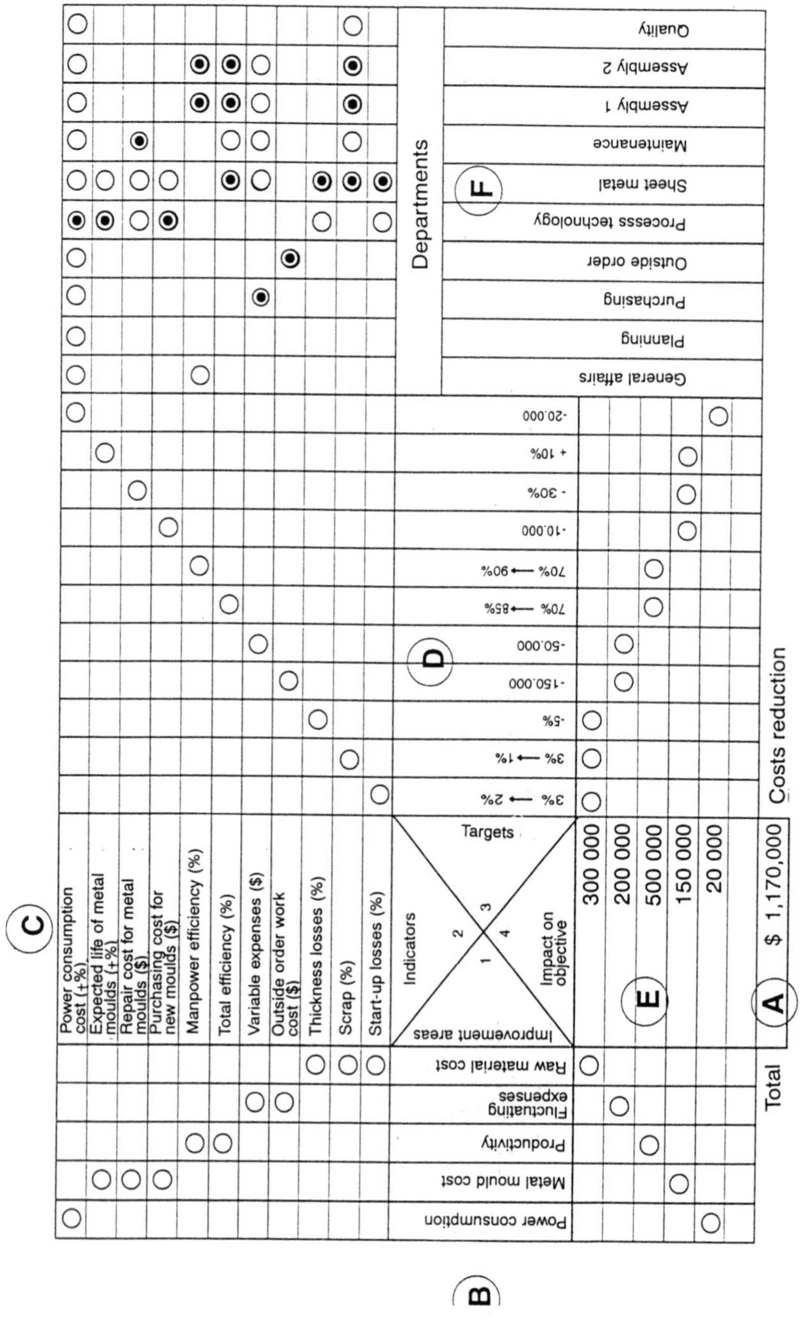

Figure 6.7   X Matrix – study case: Manufacturing cost reduction.

- Responsibilities
- Quantitative breakdown of the objective by improvement area

The X Matrix given as an example in Figure 6.7 is limited to these factors. It gives the general objective in zone A, the improvement areas in zone B, the indicators in zone C, the targets in zone D, the quantitative breakdown in zone E and the responsibilities in zone F. The empty circles represent the graphic links between the elements in the matrix. In zone F the solid circles represent "prime responsibilities" compared with the co-responsibilities represented by the empty circles.

We will now see how to prepare a first level X Matrix. Let us take Figure 6.7 as a reference. The entry point is zone A, where we insert the total quantitative value of the objective to be pursued. This can be a money value, time (for an objective to reduce Lead Time), a percentage (for example, the improvement of a qualitative parameter), etc. In our example it is the amount to be saved, i.e. $1 170 000.

Next we fill in zone B, where we put the first level improvement areas indicated in the Tree Diagram deployment (i.e. the priority areas selected). In our case they are Materials Yield, Other Costs, Productivity, Dies, Energy.

In zone C we then fill in the indicators chosen. In our example in the improvement area Materials Yield, the indicators are: "Start-up losses", "Scrap", "Thickness losses". These are linked graphically to the improvement area to which they refer by circles (or Xs).

In zone D we put the reference target (result to be obtained) for each indicator, perhaps expressed in terms of "present situation" and "objective" (from . . . , to . . .). We then insert in zone E the values corresponding to the target in terms of their contribution to the general objective, and check the coherence between the two.

In our study case we have inserted each of the financial contributions to the total savings planned. It can be seen that we have only transferred to the X Matrix the elements which were already defined when we prepared the Tree Diagram. This is of course indispensable to check that we have broken it down sufficiently, and to identify any incoherent elements or the absence (or duplication) of any steps in the logic chain.

The X Matrix is a compact document, easy to understand due to its graphic form. However, its real added value in comparison with the Tree Diagram only starts to appear when we begin to prepare zone F which concerns "Responsibilities". It is at this point that we must define the people to whom we assign responsibility for operating results. They are the people who were involved in identifying the ways chosen for tackling the objective. In the first stage of the process of organizing management, these responsibilities mainly concern carrying out the next (lower) levels of deployment. Once the whole reiterative deployment process has been completed, they can be confirmed or, if necessary, changed.

The "definitive" responsibilities are usually identified at three levels:

1   *Direct or prime responsibility* (represented by a solid circle). This is the assignment of full responsibility and leadership for the objective. The selection is made much more on the basis of competence than of the level and status of the persons concerned.

2   *Co-responsibility* (represented by an empty circle). The "co-responsible" persons or units are asked to contribute to the objective in the ways and at the times decided by those with prime responsibility (on the basis of the policies agreed during the deployment phase).

These requirements will already have been defined in terms of implementation of the deployment. These persons may be lower or higher in status than the objective leaders. The choice is made on the basis of the skills required and the opportunities to be exploited. As these are "red" objectives, the people concerned cannot refuse to take part since by definition they cannot have things to do which are more important than what is necessary to achieve the priority objectives. The only exceptions are obvious emergencies. In any case since they will be considered co-responsible for the results it is in their interest to contribute to them satisfactorily.

3   *Availability* (represented by an X). They are units or persons who can be asked to contribute to an objective in the course of achievement, depending on the problems or needs identi-

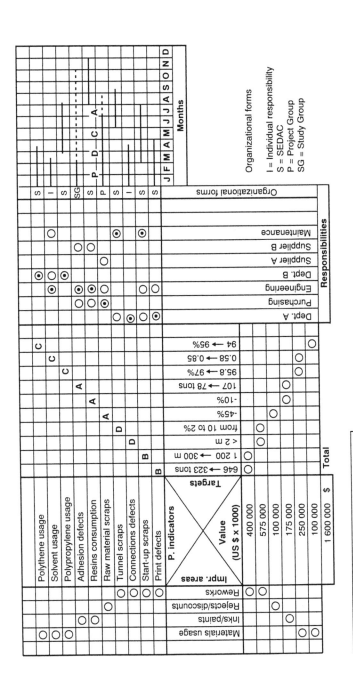

Figure 6.8 *Operational X Matrix (third level).*

fied by the objective leader. (They are contributions which are not identifiable before the start of operations.)

As mentioned earlier, the X Matrices at second and third levels are usually more specific and detailed in content. A typical layout is illustrated in Figure 6.8 which gives all the elements usually considered necessary for setting up effective operating management. The additional elements compared with the simplified version so far shown are:

- Guidelines/surrounding conditions/constraints
- Organizational arrangements planned for improvements
- Time scale for developing the improvement actions and for reaching the targets

Guidelines/Surrounding Conditions/Constraints

They are elements useful for the definition of the ways agreed on for the pursuit of the objectives, to ensure that they are coherent (see Chapter 2 on planning). Some examples of guidelines and constraints are given in Figure 6.8 (in the box at the bottom).

Organizational Arrangements Planned for Improvements

These normally fall into the following categories: individual tasks, group projects, SEDAC operations, study groups. These are described here, together with the criteria for their selection according to the type of objective or action to be carried out. In Figure 6.8 it can be seen how the form chosen is set out in the X Matrix.

Individual Tasks

The responsibility for achieving the target of the project, or for carrying out the specific action required is assigned to a single person. This is the most common form used and is recommended when the actions or projects have a high specialist/technical content, or in the case of relatively simple actions or objectives.

Project Groups

Groups of three to seven persons, usually middle managers from different functions, selected to tackle an improvement project.

They use the problem-finding and problem-solving methodologies of the PDCA process. They meet regularly (usually every one or two weeks), coordinated by a leader who either has been previously appointed or has been elected by the group. The group is dissolved at the end of the project (which should not last more than four to six months, because of the risk of losing its effectiveness). Project Groups should only be used for innovative or complex projects since they are usually cumbersome and time-consuming.

Study Groups

These are made up of senior managers or persons of outstanding competence, and are almost always multifunctional. They are used when it is not clear how an objective should be tackled and an investigation is necessary to arrive at a decision. It is a first phase organization which should lead to one of the three other types of organization described, depending on the approach selected. This phase should not last more than a month.

Action SEDAC

This form of organization is probably the most modern and effective (it is used by almost all the firms quoted in the first part of the book as examples of success). This does not mean that it can be used universally. It is used when the performance of existing activities must be improved, through the upgrading of the operating methods already in use in the firm. It is not suitable for innovative projects (for which Project Groups are recommended). It is the type of organization which ought to be the most common after Individual Tasks, since it concerns the most common type of improvement. Many of the projects which firms assign today to Project Groups or Improvement Groups would be better handled by this type of organization.

Experience demonstrates that by using this approach the effectiveness of improvement activities could be increased tenfold. It is certainly true that the time taken to develop a project using Action SEDAC is about a third of that taken by a group. A SEDAC project takes two or three months compared with the three to six months which are the statistical range for a Project Group.

Time Scale for Developing the Improvement and for Reaching Targets

For management to be effective, it is necessary to plan the times for each target or organizational programme. The projects/actions can be planned to run in parallel or in series, depending on the assessment of what is possible or advantageous. Remember that if the actions are to be carried out by the same people, it is more effective to plan, for example, two blocks of five actions in sequence rather than all 10 in parallel (effectiveness through focusing). The contents of the timetable vary according to the organizational arrangement selected:

- If it is an Individual Task, the complete implementation time should be planned
- If it is a Project Group, its development phases should be planned (possibly using PDCA)
- If it is a SEDAC, the time necessary to achieve the objective should be planned; in fact, although it has the same nature as a project, SEDAC carries out the PDCA phases in parallel
- If it is a Study Group, the time assigned to the study and the planning of implementation should be planned

Visual Management Using the SEDAC System

As already indicated, the X Matrix shown above forms the "bridge" between an objective and its operational management. As we have already said, effective operational management is based on the "Visual Management" of the entire process launched to achieve the priority objectives.

The instruments proposed for this purpose are Master SEDAC and Sub SEDAC. These are part of the SEDAC system developed by the Deming prizewinner Ryuji Fukuda, which also includes Operating SEDAC (see below).

The objective of Master and Sub SEDAC is to provide all the elements required for the Visual Management of the performance indicators to be improved and of all the improvement activities which aim to achieve the planned objectives. These instruments are the practical application of the fundamental principle of Breakthrough management, which states that "the main task of managers at all levels is to work every day on the priority objectives of the business, concentrating on the bottlenecks to the process on which their achievement depends". These instruments do in fact overcome the main obstacles to the application of this principle, namely through the possibility to Manage by Priorities and to identify the bottlenecks and the critical path leading to the priority objectives. Let us now see how Master and Sub SEDAC help us to manage visually by priority. We shall then see how they help us to identify and manage the bottlenecks.

Master SEDAC is the graphical tool for managing the objectives contained in the first level X Matrix. It contains the synthesis of the objectives which contribute to the responsibilities of the head of an operating unit or a Breakthrough objective. The Master SEDAC is drawn up starting from the indicators and targets of the first level X Matrix. In the same way there is a Sub SEDAC for each second and third level X Matrix.

The number of Master and Sub SEDACs, and the number of X Matrices coincide only in theory, however. The former are in fact only drawn up for the indicators or objectives to which it is sensible to apply Visual Management. Note the typical pattern of a Master and a Sub SEDAC in Figure 6.9 and their link with a scheme of Effective Management in Figure 6.10 (the meaning of the cards on the SEDAC branches will be explained later).

SEDAC is laid out graphically on a board (say 1m × 2m) visible to all in the office of the manager responsible for the objective, or in the workplace where it must be applied. It is usually a "fishbone" diagram with the indicator of the main objective on the right and those of the sub-objectives (targets) on the left. There are, however, other forms of graph which can be used according to the type of objective.

To ensure Effective Management, the indicator of the overall objective (the "planned" result) should be updated weekly or monthly. The other indicators, of both Master and Sub SEDACs, should be updated at least weekly if not daily. The company information system is probably incapable of providing the summaries or the breakdowns required to measure the performances to be monitored. Indeed, information systems are usually

Tree Diagram

"X" Matrix

Master SEDAC

Sub SEDAC

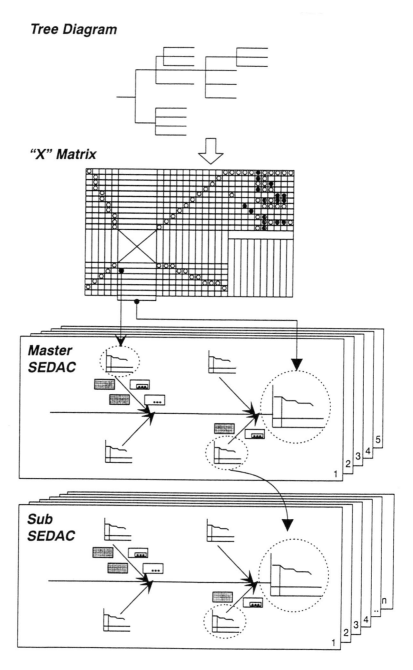

Figure 6.9 *Setting up Master and Sub SEDACs.*

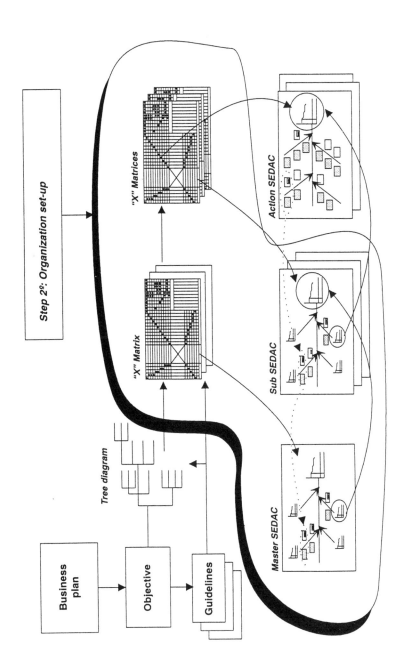

Figure 6.10 *The Effective Management cycle: Organization set-up.*

only designed to report on results whereas the information which we require concerns causes rather than results. In any case it is difficult to obtain them on a daily basis. If it exists, so much the better! Otherwise, in the majority of cases, the data will be collected "manually".

The fact of having to collect and record data manually every day about our own objectives does have the advantage of ensuring that we stay in close contact with them. In practice they are usually monitored in this way, even in highly computerized companies. It must, however, be remembered that this only consists of a simple sum to be calculated each day for each of one's "right hand" SEDAC indicators. The others are updated "bottom-up" by the managers at the next level down. The Master SEDAC for our study case and one of its Sub SEDACs are illustrated in Figure 6.11. In this case the Master SEDAC is the management tool of the factory manager, and the Sub SEDACs belong to his or her departmental managers.

So far we have been concerned with organizing the Visual Management of the indicators and the projects to be supervised. In the following two paragraphs we shall see how these instruments connect with the organizational arrangements created to implement the improvements, and in particular how they are used for operating management.

IMPROVEMENT ACTIVITIES

Operating SEDAC is the key methodology of the operational phase of the approach illustrated. Action SEDAC is the final element required to complete the Breakthrough management process proposed in this book. As can be seen in Figure 6.12, it provides the tool for transforming the two previous phases of "planning" and "organizing management" into operating reality. It is directly plugged into the cascade down from the Master SEDAC and Sub SEDACs which are its origin. Action SEDAC belongs to the family of SEDAC system instruments developed by Ryuji Fukuda. SEDAC*, as already mentioned, is an acronym

---

* The copyright of the SEDAC system for Europe and South America is the property of Galgano & Associates.

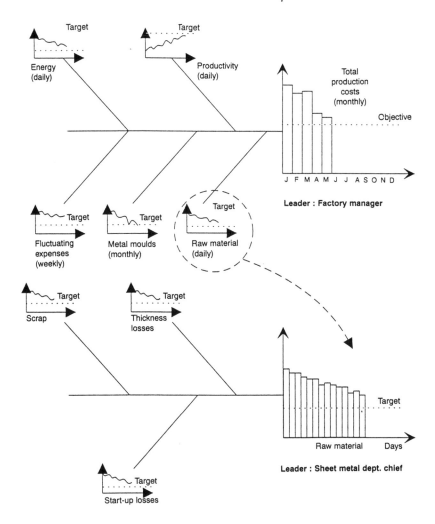

Figure 6.11 *Master and Sub SEDAC in the study case.*

derived from Structure for Enhancing Daily Activities through Creativity.

The operating system is based on the generous use of post-it type cards. The operating tools of the system (Action SEDAC) consist of various types of diagram called "SEDAC Diagrams". These are boards on view in the offices or departments where the problem is to be eliminated or the performance to be improved.

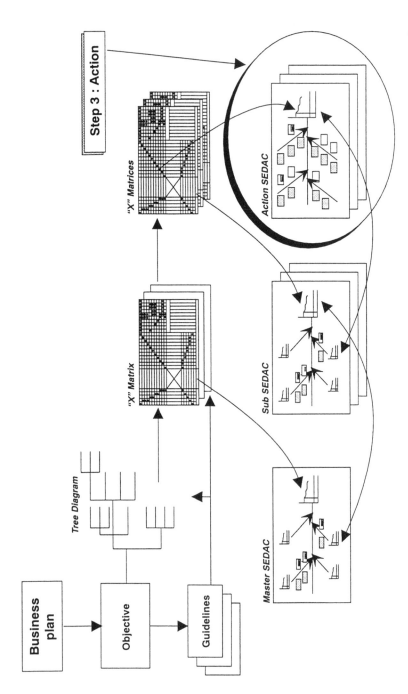

Figure 6.12   The Effective Management cycle: Action.

In Breakthrough management the point of departure for a SEDAC Diagram is the lowest level indicator identified in the deployment process, that is an indicator and target from a branch of a Sub SEDAC. In our study case it could, for example, be attached to the objective "start-up losses". The link with the Sub SEDAC and the Master SEDAC which are its source is illustrated in Figure 6.13.

There are various forms of SEDAC diagrams designed for different types of objective, such as:

- CEDAC* (cause-and-effect diagram with addition of cards – Figure 6.14). The most widely-used diagram, designed to highlight cause-and-effect relationships, i.e. the problems and obstacles in the way of the improvement sought after
- PERTAC (a combination of SEDAC and PERT Diagram – Figure 6.15). Very useful for customized processes (engineering or production) where it is necessary to concentrate on critical paths
- FLOWAC (a combination of SEDAC and a flow diagram – Figure 6.16). Recommended where the improvement concerns a process or a procedure

Of all the SEDAC Diagrams, the most widely employed is certainly CEDAC. We will now use it to illustrate how a SEDAC Diagram works physically.

The CEDAC Diagram(**)

The CEDAC Diagram is a methodology which enables the improvement process to be brought to the work station and to be part of the everyday life of managers, foremen and the work force. It also makes it possible to involve a large number of people in the improvement activities with only a minimum of meetings.

---

* The copyright for the CEDAC Diagram for Europe is the property of Galgano & Associates and for Great Britain, France and USA of Productivity Inc.
** Section written by Carlalberto Da Pozzo, Galgano & Associates.

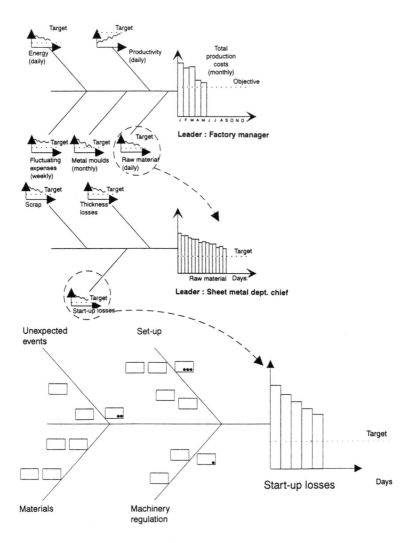

Figure 6.13   *SEDACs in cascade in the study case.*

The CEDAC Diagram is a very flexible instrument which can be used to manage a variety of situations:

• Organization and definition of the individual improvement activities

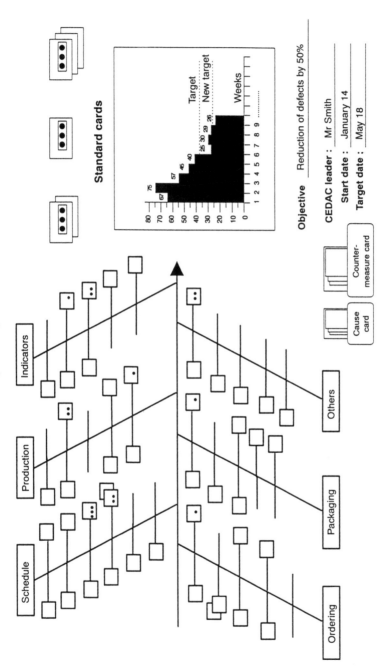

Figure 6.14 *CEDAC Diagram of "shipment problem".*

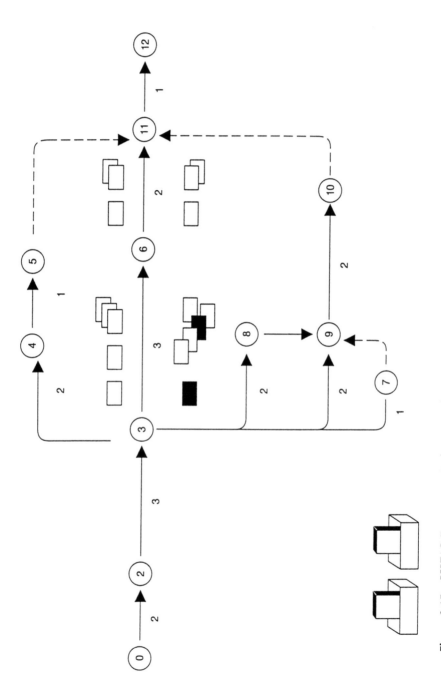

Figure 6.15   PERTAC (Programme, Evaluation and Review Technique + SEDAC).

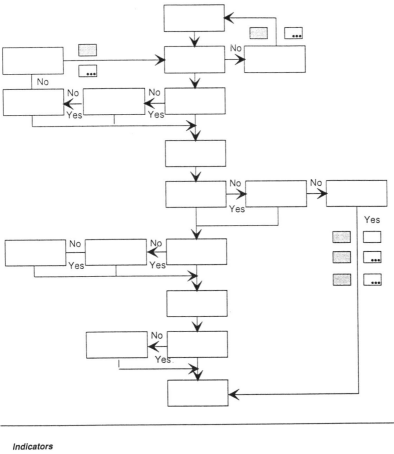

Figure 6.16 *Flow diagram + SEDAC (Flow–AC).*

- Supervision and continuous improvement of operating performances
- Improvement projects (when not purely innovative)
- Standardization of improvement

Physically the CEDAC Diagram is a board located at the spot where the problem has to be solved or the activity improved. The board must be visible to all, and everyone must have access to it. It is divided into two parts (Figure 6.17): the "effects" side and the "causes" (or "levers") side. On the effects side we put the most suitable indicators for monitoring the problem or objective ("the object of improvement"). These are usually in the form of graphs updated daily. This allows all interested parties to have the performance improvement trend constantly in view. On the causes/levers side we put the elements which prevent the improvement or create the problem and also ideas on how to solve it. Anyone can indicate on cards what the obstacles are that he or she has found which prevent the improvement from taking place and/or what remedies could be applied to overcome them. These notes are made on different coloured cards (indicating cause or remedy).

The leader responsible for the project or objective will test the ideas which he or she finds the most interesting. The results of these experiments will be evaluated using the indicators which monitor the problem. If the ideas are successful, the improvement is obvious to all. In other words, the CEDAC Diagram makes it possible to:

- Call the attention of everyone constantly to an important problem or target that the firm wants to tackle (identified through Effective Management deployment)
- Collect a large amount of information about the real causes of a problem or obstacles to an improvement
- Stimulate the generation, collection and consideration of the ideas of a number of people without having to call meetings
- Inform everyone in real time about the improvements under way and about the introduction of new standards

The setting up and administration of the CEDAC Diagram is carried out in seven basic phases, some concerning the effects side and others the causes/levers side (Figure 6.17). These phases are:

1   Identifying the parameters to be used for measuring the results of the improvement actions and their impact on the objective (the indicators)

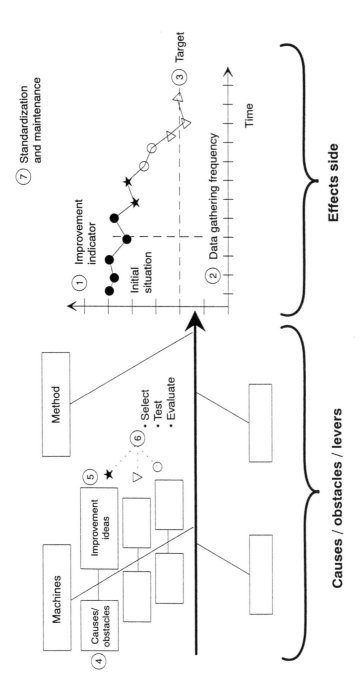

Figure 6.17   *Setting up a CEDAC Diagram.*

2   Defining the frequency of data collection for the indicators
3   Defining the objectives (targets) for the indicators
4   Collecting the cards concerning the obstacles/problems (the reasons which prevent the target from being reached)
5   Collecting the cards with the improvement ideas (how to overcome the problems/obstacles)
6   Selecting and testing the improvement ideas (trying out what appear to be the most valid ideas)
7   Defining and applying the new standards (to make the improvements irreversible)

The CEDAC board is administered by a "CEDAC leader" (who is responsible for that specific CEDAC). He or she is the person to whom the top management has assigned the problem or improvement to be tackled and plays a decisive role in the correct use of the diagram and in the effective application of the improvement process.

The CEDAC leader is responsible for organizing and managing the diagram and coordinating all related activities. He or she should have a detailed knowledge of the problem/improvement area, and be a leader both in status and in his or her personal qualities. The main tasks are to:

• Promote the activity
• Design and organize the board
• Analyze the obstacle cards
• Evaluate the improvement idea cards (see Figure 6.18)
• Test the improvement ideas considered suitable (eventually with other units)
• Standardize the effective ideas

It is important to emphasize that the CEDAC leader does not have to do all this him or herself, but he or she must be able to ensure that each phase is carried out correctly, using whoever he or she thinks most suitable. The advantages of the CEDAC Diagram can be seen from these points of view:

1   *The large number of people involved.* The diagram makes everyone aware of an important problem or objective, and attracts their attention and involvement (quite apart from taking an

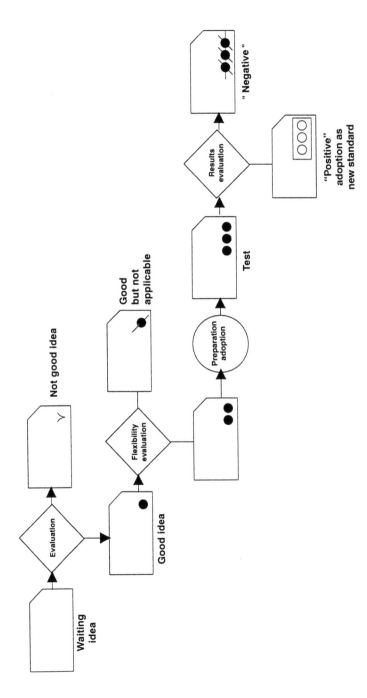

Figure 6.18   *Card evaluation scheme.*

active part by putting cards on the board). It stimulates and brings together everyone's ideas on the problem and its solution, and the dynamics of the process do a great deal to integrate the various levels and functions (including staff and line). The diagram is visible to all and everyone has access to the definition of standards. It stimulates and generates a large volume of inputs into the diagnosis and the improvement activity.

2 *The operating method.* Since it takes cause-and-effect relationships as its focal point the method continuously consolidates this approach in practice. It provides everyone with immediate feedback on the results obtained and creates a concrete, immediate sense of achievement. Everyone involved knows the process which has developed the standards, and how they affect the parameters of the process. Finally, it helps to diffuse the new standards.

3 *The development of the improvement culture.* Since it develops the concept of continuous improvement on a daily basis, the diagram helps to integrate improvement and day-to-day tasks, so that improvement becomes a normal, routine activity. The CEDAC Diagram is the basic tool for implementing the Breakthrough management process.

MONITORING AND MANAGING

The Approach

Of the four phases of Breakthrough management (planning/programming, organizing management, operating, monitoring and management), it is the last phase, monitoring and management, which converts all the potential created in the other phases into "Breakthrough management". This is the dynamic stage which brings to life all the instruments previously set up. It transforms the scheme in Figure 6.1 into an operating management system. No new tools or methodologies are introduced at this stage. It is simply a question of organizing what has already been created so that it focuses on the projected Breakthrough.

The management objective is therefore to build an effective system for monitoring and managing operating activities which makes it possible to:

- Manage priorities in "real time" (day by day)
- Monitor the priority objective indicators "visually"
- Identify current bottlenecks which are preventing objectives from being achieved
- Manage the bottlenecks effectively

Let us see how this objective can be achieved. As we have already said, "real time" information is the condition of Breakthrough management. The information flow for this purpose is based on the cascade framework of SEDAC and transports the management information to the right places in the following way.

Updating Management Information

This is done using an implosive type of information flow with consolidations at each level upwards through the organization, going in the opposite direction to the deployment flow of the indicators (i.e. from the particular to the general, see Figure 6.19). This means that either daily or weekly each SEDAC leader has to update the indicator linked to his or her objective simultaneously on two graphs: the right hand side of "his or her" SEDAC and that of the branch of the Sub SEDAC from which it stemmed.

The same will happen between the Sub SEDAC and the Master SEDAC. Similar information must be provided by the other improvement organization tools such as Project Groups and Individual Tasks. The information can be transmitted upward in various ways, by computer network (if available), photocopy, fax, telephone and direct recording on the diagram of the level above.

The type of flow is illustrated on the right side of Figure 6.19. This updating process allows the Master and Sub SEDAC leaders to check day by day which performance is the most critical and, by using the cascade, what are the causes. By following the indicators critical path they are able to identify which is the area

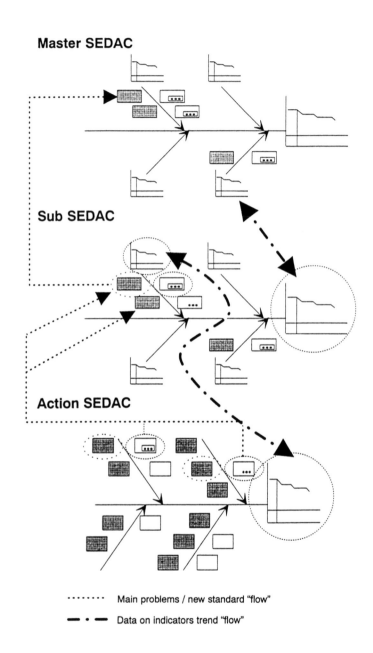

Figure 6.19   *Information flow.*

currently most critical to the priority objective, and move in on precisely those bottlenecks which must be the priorities of the moment.

Information on Problems/Ideas/New Standards

At the same time as they transmit performance data for the indicators, the SEDAC and Sub SEDAC leaders are also asked to send information regarding major obstacles, the main ideas and new standards introduced. This allows objectives leaders at the next level up to have "real time" information on the main problems arising, what is being done about them, and what new standards have been introduced, all without waiting for reports (always late) or calling meetings (always costly and difficult to organize). The bottom-up flow of this type of information is illustrated on the left side of Figure 6.19.

Information on Improvement Activities

This can be partly extrapolated from the previous flow. If major problems have actually been reported, it is highly likely that some remedies can be found. All the better if important ideas/remedies or even new standards have already been identified. Another type of information which we need is the number of obstacle cards and idea cards collected. This is transmitted at the same time as the previous information, and gives an idea as to whether and to what extent the improvement activity is under way. The information is very important for Breakthrough management. We have already seen how much this depends on the "upstream management" of what can generate the desired improvement to the outputs. So, if it is true that by selecting indicators measuring causes and not results, management can concentrate on the variables which determine the desired result, it will be even more effective if it can concentrate on the activities which aim to make those improvements. It is hopeless to expect the performance of the "cause" variables to improve if there is no improvement activity aimed at doing so.

It is evident that this management approach allows results to be managed "two steps upstream" (that is by managing the activities which can improve the performance of the causes which determine the performance that we want to improve). It therefore ensures greater effectiveness (because it is acting on the improvement levers of the causes) and quicker results (because it acts earlier). One could add that it manages yet another step upstream, by identifying the problems or obstacles which must be removed if improvement is to take place.

How can we improve performance if we do not know what to tackle? It is not by accident that the Japanese call the problems "treasures". If we did not first dig out the problems, we should not be able to launch any improvement activity, since we should not know what to aim at. Knowing this we can perhaps understand the reasons for the great success of Japanese industry, which as an institution is focused on the improvement of the process variables which produce business results, through the fanatical removal of the slightest problem. It should also enable us to understand better the real difference between management and management control: the former is focused on causes, the latter on results.

Finally it should be remembered that for the complete improvement process to be managed visually, the bottom-up information cards should also carry information on the improvement activities taking place outside SEDAC (through Project Groups, Individual Tasks, etc.).

OPERATING MANAGEMENT

"Operating management" is the point in the Breakthrough management process which brings into use all the potential created in the preceding phases, including monitoring. It should let us identify the bottlenecks of the moment which are getting in the way of the priority objectives, and take the right measures to remove them. Using the proposed system we can pursue the first of these objectives through a mixture of several operating methods:

- Management by "critical indicators"
- Management by "critical flows"
- "Patrol"

Management by Critical Indicators

The process is illustrated by the following possible situation. The Master SEDAC leader (the factory manager in our example) will make a monthly check of total production costs on the right hand indicator of his Master SEDAC, to check the coherence between the improvement made and therefore the results expected, and the actual results achieved. Discrepancies would probably call into question the validity of the deployment itself, and could lead to the decision to revise it. But his or her main task is what he or she does weekly or daily, which is to check the progress of the sub-indicators entered on his or her Master SEDAC. It is in this way that he or she can be aware of the most critical indicator of the moment in relation to planned results. He or she will then detach the graph (usually an A4 sheet) which indicates the critical performance and go to see its leader (of the Sub SEDAC concerned) so that they can assess together the reasons for the sub-standard improvement.

Together they will try to spot the most critical sub-indicator in the Sub SEDAC (probably already "assessed" by its leader), and so on, until in an Action SEDAC they identify the main cause of the problem or sub-performance. We shall see later what the leaders should do once they have arrived at the problem.

Management by Critical Flow

The Master SEDAC leader must also make a daily examination of the information coming in from the problems/ideas/new standards cards (the main ones and the quantitative data). If the operating indicators discussed above do not show any relative problems (i.e. one of them worse than the others), the bottleneck of the moment must be sought out using this type of information. The following situations may be found:

1 *An insufficient flow of cards (or even none).* It is clear that in this case it would be difficult for performance to improve. If there has been an improvement, it is probably because of the greater attention focused on it as being performance "under observation". This is, however, a particularly

"delicate" situation. If the improvement is not due to any specific change, it will probably disappear as soon as it is no longer under a spotlight. Therefore something must be done, but what is the bottleneck? It is probably the leaders at operating level who do not know how to get an improvement process going. It is on them and on their capacity to create participation that he or she must concentrate.

2   *Only "obstacles" cards.* In this case he or she must find ways of stimulating the diagnostic skills, the creativity or the improvement organization capabilities of the line management concerned (later we shall see how this can be done).

3   *Only "obstacles" and "ideas" cards, but no new standards.* In this case the leaders are probably failing to move the organization in order to implement the ideas, or else the ideas are very weak (in which case, back to the previous case).

4   *Cards with obstacles or ideas to which the experience or know-how of the senior leaders can make a contribution.* In this case the "boss" joins in and takes part in the improvement activities directly on the spot, as a consultant.

5   *Some of the standards introduced are considered risky.* These are situations which the leaders consider they must "freeze" since they are potentially damaging, usually for reasons well known to them.

"Patrol"

This is an activity with a flow opposite to those above, being carried out bottom-up instead of top-down. It is performed weekly or monthly by every Master or Sub SEDAC leader (including the top manager of the operating unit) to help the organization in its improvement activities from the bottom (to "improve its improvement capabilities"). This sort of operation, besides showing commitment to the activity and the objective, aims to bring concrete help to the weak links in the organization.

These weak links are mainly identified by assessing the activities of each Action SEDAC during systematic "patrols" of the operating sections (production and offices). The main activity is to coach the middle managers involved in the improvement activities, but it is not unusual to come across genuinely important operating problems or improvement opportunities.

The methods for managing the bottleneck discovered by these means must be found through analysis of the nature of the problem. In the firms which have gone furthest in the use of the SEDAC system, this is systematically carried out through "Window Analysis". At Sony, for example, it is considered to be the basic mechanism for Breakthrough management. There are simpler ways of doing it based on the professional capacities of the managers involved, which can in the first instance replace such a "scientific" approach. The purpose of the diagnosis is to identify the nature of the problem or obstacle which is creating the bottleneck. In fact its removal or remedy depends a great deal on this diagnosis, as the following examples show:

- If the cause of the problem is not known we must immediately set up a Study Group to tackle it (or even better a task force in the case of a priority objective)
- If it is already known in the firm how to avoid the problem but not in the area in question, the method must be properly explained to its staff
- If, on the other hand, everyone knows in theory how to avoid the problem, but in practice they fail to do so, adequate training of the staff is required
- If it is an improvement which is not being tackled properly in terms of method, it is probably necessary to set up a specific Action SEDAC or other form of organization

Let us simplify the description of this important moment for management, that is "how to tackle priority bottlenecks", by giving a few practical recipes which can be used if the complete operating system is based on SEDAC Diagrams. Let us examine them according to the causes which the manager may have to face when he or she identifies the bottleneck:

1 *A large number of problems/obstacles have been reported on the bottleneck* (for example, a large number of cards on the left side of the CEDAC branch), but without any improvement ideas. In this case the manager should be able to establish:

- *Whether the problem/obstacle is really unknown.* Then he or she should straight away set up a study task force, involving everyone necessary, at whatever level. This is possible because of the level in the structure of the Master SEDAC leader, and is justified by the importance of the problem (the bottleneck of a business priority).
- *Whether there are no ideas because of the weakness of the Action SEDAC leader.* In this case the Master SEDAC leader must try to understand whether it is through a lack of commitment, motivation or capacity, and take action in consequence. In the last case (incapacity) he or she should focus on how to help the leader, and not show up his or her inadequacies (that can come later . . . the immediate priority is how best to tackle the problem!).

2 *On the bottleneck both obstacles and ideas considered valid are recorded but these have not been tested, or the remedies demonstrated to be valid have not been engineered or applied because of the slowness of one or other of the units involved* (for example Purchasing, Accounts, Organization, Tooling, etc.). In the SEDAC Diagrams these situations are identified by one, two or three circles on the remedies/ideas cards. Analysis is therefore very easy.

   In this case the authority and status of the Master SEDAC leader should be used to start up what has not yet been activated, bypassing normal procedures if necessary ("the priority end justifies the exceptional means").

3 *On the bottleneck (the entire Action SEDAC or one of its branches) there are no problems/obstacles or idea cards.* In this case the problem is similar to the first one, but much more serious. The diagnosis is very simple: the Action SEDAC leader is failing to deal with the problem. Very probably what he or she is basically lacking is the capacity to involve his or her staff in the improvement process, although his or her own diagnostic capacity could also be a problem (otherwise he or she would at least have found something!).

   A major or drastic remedy is required: either the SEDAC leader is switched, or the Master SEDAC leader dedicates all the time that may be necessary to help him or her (for

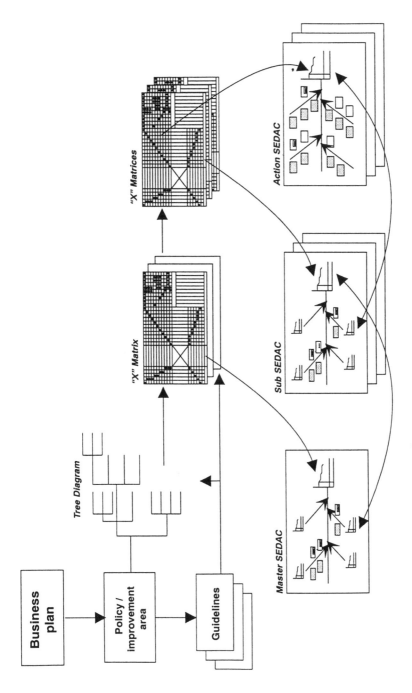

Figure 6.20   The Effective Management cycle.

example, one or two hours a day for at least a week). It will be worth it, as we are talking about a priority problem!

It can be seen that what is proposed makes a minimum use of meetings or working groups (but when it does, the result is very effective) or of paperwork, accounting or EDP systems. Instead it is based on management:

- In real time
- Focused on the causes/levers of the problems/improvements (and not on the results)
- Attacking the bottlenecks of the objectives
- Free so far as possible from bureaucratic procedures and the constraints of the management hierarchy
- Capable of using the skills required at the right moment

This system, even in its most "naive" form as presented here, should make it easier to meet what we stated at the beginning of this paragraph to be the requirement of effective operating management, that is:

- *Being capable of managing priorities "in real time"* (through the continuous supervision of the operating indicators monitoring the variables of the business processes concerned)
- *Being capable of "visual supervision" of the indicators of the priority objectives* (which is possible thanks to the SEDAC cascade system)
- *Being capable of spotting the current bottlenecks blocking the priority objectives* (through the methodologies provided for this purpose by the SEDAC system)
- *Being capable of dealing effectively with the bottlenecks* (thanks to the Window Analysis methodology or its substitutes)

This completes our description of the last phase of the Breakthrough management process, which we have called "monitoring and management". It should now be more clear what the methods are which translate the Breakthrough management framework proposed into practice, and which we will reproduce again (see Figure 6.20).

7
The Whole Management System

As I mentioned in Chapter 1 on the Breakthrough approach, this book describes exceptional management methods. The connections between these special mechanisms and more systematic management methods have already been dealt with, however. I mentioned in the Introduction that any one of the specific instruments (Planning by Priorities, Effective Management and Business Process Reengineering (BPR)) may become a very good way to introduce operative mechanisms normally employed in the best companies today. What is proposed here is perhaps the ideal way to introduce them. This is based on the following considerations:

1 It is always wise to introduce new management mechanisms through significant experimentation.
2 It is not always easy to find within a company energies ready and available for the introduction of something new that does not necessarily respond to existing needs.

These are the very characteristics of the Breakthrough approach proposed in this book. In fact

• Concentration is on aspects that are significant by definition, because the method is applied to important problems and objectives

- Existing energies are exploited, as the approach is used in support of objectives and problems the company already has to face

Due to the entrepreneurial and practical spirit of this book I have chosen to concentrate on the operating aspects rather than on strategic planning and company business. The following are two opportunities for developing a more evolved management system through the adoption of the mechanisms analyzed in this book:

1 In practice BPR prepares a company for the introduction of Management by Processes and Day to Day Management (DDM).
2 Effective Management acts as the perfect threshold to Management by Policy (MBP).

The managerial model made up of these three operative dimensions, typical of leading companies today, is briefly described in this chapter.

THE REFERENCE MANAGEMENT SYSTEM

The reference model emerging nowadays is clearly defined. The ways to implement it are more diverse (and rightly so), and therefore less easy to codify. To give you an idea of the changes that are occurring in managerial methods I will quote two examples: one is a commercial concern operating in the consumer electronics sector, while the other is a finance services company.

Here is what the general manager of the commercial concern has written:

I honestly would not know how to manage my firm in the present scenario if I could not use Management by Policy and Management by Processes. In particular I would be at a loss to know otherwise how to mobilize all my collaborators on the company priorities of the moment. There is only one problem: these mechanisms compel us to think like entrepreneurs instead of managers. But perhaps that is the explanation of the successes we are obtaining!

And this is what the director general of the financial company says:

How did we manage to find out before whether our clients were satisfied, how to identify problems that penalized our service, improve the performances of our business processes? We didn't even know properly what these processes were! Today, with Management by Processes all that has become normal routine!

These words sum up excellently the characteristics of the managerial system that is becoming established today, giving the feeling of just how innovative its mechanisms are. And now, what is the rationale behind this system and what are these mechanisms?

THE NEW MANAGERIAL MODEL

The model of the new managerial system is divided into three operative dimensions (Figure 7.1):

1   Management by Policy (MBP)
2   Day to Day Management (DDM)
3   Management by Processes

The labels given to these dimensions vary slightly from sector to sector and company to company. The following are some points to help put into focus these different dimensions:

1   *Management by Policy.* This expression refers to the present trend regarding the evolutions that Management by Objectives (MBO) and Management Control are undergoing. In particular, MBP is a fusion of MBO with the new operating management approaches, oriented towards greater entrepreneurship. An important aspect is that it focuses on a very limited number of objectives, which are identified by starting from company priorities, and the principal objective is to supervise their operating management.
    It should be remembered that one of the basic points of Management by Objectives was, on the contrary, to "give

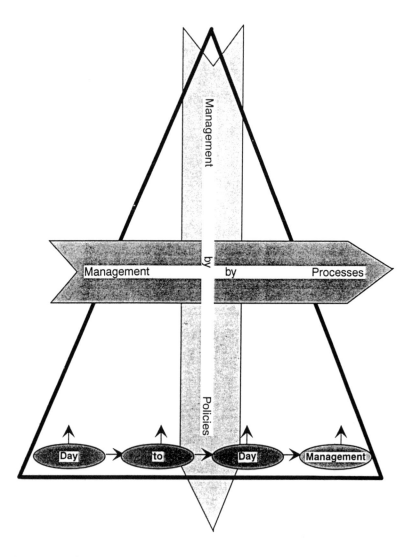

Figure 7.1   *The management reference model.*

objectives to all the managers", so as to evaluate their performance and organize the rewarding system.
2   *Day to Day Management*. This is a direct descendant of Total
    Quality and organizes the supervision of the company's bot-
    tom-up continuous improvement process. The innovation is

that the process is introduced as a systematic fact, and is managed by the line in a bottom-up manner.

3 *Management by Processes.* This means managing and improving by business processes as well as by functions. It is an increasingly widespread instrument, especially in service companies where, together with upside-down pyramid concepts (the organization in the service of the front line), it is becoming the most important dimension.

The recent reorganizational approaches based on BPR and illustrated in Chapter 4, encourage this need as a natural evolution of the new organizing approach that must later be managed with coherence in daily practice. I will now give you a more comprehensive description of the three dimensions of the model.

MANAGEMENT BY POLICY

As I have already said, this management dimension is the natural evolution of the Effective Management system described in Chapter 6. It is a simple matter to transform the approach presented there into a systematic method of managing company priorities through the hierarchical line. MBP is called Hoshin Kanri in Japanese. Ryuji Fukuda introduces the theme in the following terms:

> *in the sixties, we [the Japanese] were very good at carrying out improvement activities (Kaizen), but not at focusing them on the business priorities. In the West you were very good at identifying priorities and objectives (through management by objectives), but did not succeed in involving the whole company in their pursuit. In the years from 1970 to 1980, we Japanese have combined the two (the Japanese and Western approaches) with the logic of managing by priorities, creating a new, better management approach – Management by Policy.*

From a more technical viewpoint, MBP is defined as the management mechanism (developed from management by objectives) which:

- Implements the entrepreneurial logic of "Managing by Priorities, while respecting in the short term the long-term policies of the company"

- Carries out "effective" planning, translating strategic plans into coherent actions for the medium term (business plan) and the short term (day by day), managed and monitored continuously
- Develops the management system, organization and culture necessary to make Total Quality operational inside the company

Its principal characteristics can be identified as being:

- Linked directly to the strategic and business plans (objectives)
- Focused on a small number of basic priorities (between one and three, chosen annually by top management) with major objectives
- Joint identification of the objectives and measures necessary to obtain the desired results ("how" more important than "how much")
- A highly integrated cross-functional process focused on producing these results
- Top-down and bottom-up synergy of the management processes
- Continuous, systematic management of the process, focusing on pursuit of the objectives
- Rigorous application of the Plan, Do, Check, Act (PDCA) method
- Emphasis on cause-and-effect relationships
- Direct audits by management

Since MBP is a development of MBO, it is possible to identify the differences between the two systems. The Japanese Union of Scientists and Engineers' (JUSE) conclusions are shown in Figure 7.2. Figure 7.3, also developed by the JUSE, is the reference chart of the mechanisms of MBP, seen as an annual cycle.

From an operational viewpoint, MBP uses the "Policy Deployment" methodology, whose approach is based on a cascade of control points and check items, which follows a hierarchical logic of cause-and-effect relationships (Figure 7.4). In the West, "policy" has been defined under the following headings:

	MBO (Management by Objectives)	MBP (Management by Policies)
1. Basics	1. - Behavioural theories - Scoring system	1. - Quality Control - Control Cycle
2. Organization	2. - Focused on the individual	2. - Focused on the organiza- tion and groups of individuals
3. Operating system	3. - Decisions on objectives ("trouble-shooting system") - Planning the coherence between individuals' objectives	3. - PDCA trouble-shooting cycle - Management by Processes - Top-down/bottom-up flows
4. Priority objectives	4. - Profits/costs - Objectives expressed in terms of profit and/or cost	4. - Quality (customer satisfaction/fitness for purpose) - Global objectives on: quality, profit/cost/service
5. Approach and management	5. - Continuous pressure on objectives - Pragmatic approach: top down or participative, as needed	5. - Emphasis on processes and on flexibilities - Systematic participation by all
6. Evaluation of performance	6. - Based on results - Related to personnel management: . Selection on the basis of results . Evaluation of the job . Score system . Link with remuneration	6. - Based more on "how" (process) than on results - Integrated onto line mana- gement . Audit by the director/ manager . Self-evaluation of results/ objectives differences . Evaluation by internal customers and colleagues - No direct link with personnel management
7. Operating methods	7. - Based on "performance indicators" - The management of quality and industrial engineering are considered "subsystems"	7. - Policy deployment system - Based on "control points" - The instruments of quality control and engineering are fundamental

Figure 7.2 *Comparison of Management by Policies (MBP) vs Management by Objectives (MBO). (Source: JUSE.)*

- Long-term policy
- Annual policy
- "Campaign" policy

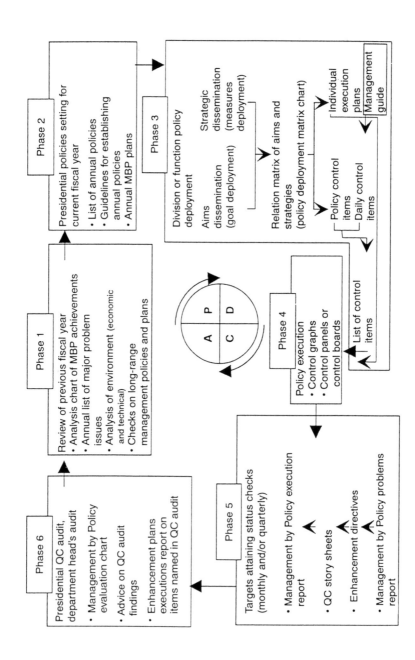

Figure 7.3 Management by Policy mechanism (the Japanese approach).

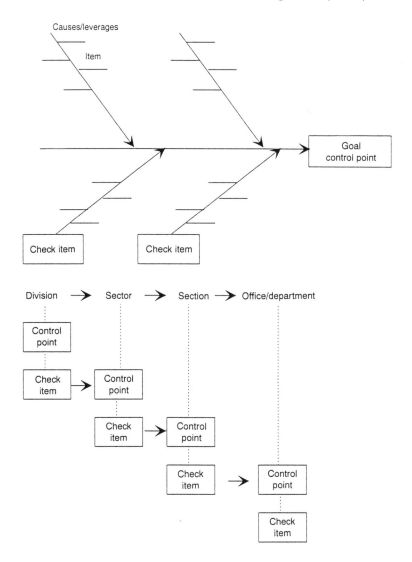

Figure 7.4 *Management by Policies – Management by Control Points.*

Long-term Policy

The long-term policy is the statement of a collection of values and principles to guide the strategic plans, the business plan and all the basic activities of the company for a number of years. Its contents are of the following type:

- Statement of the mission of the company
- Strategic principles for the pursuit of Total Quality
- Principles for customer/market relationships
- Principles for supplier relationships
- Principles for employees' role
- Cultural and organizational principles
- Reference principles for the development of the main business processes

Annual policy

This is the deployment of targets ("what") and guidelines/measures ("how") to steer the management processes and improvement activities towards the objectives of the business plan/strategic plan. It is stated on a periodic basis (yearly or every six or three months in the most dynamic Japanese companies).

Campaign Policy

Campaigns of a general nature (corporate, divisional, functional), which focus on common guidelines for all corporate improvement activities in these areas, and for those individuals not directly involved in the operating policy deployment. Examples of annual campaigns are cost reduction, improvement of product quality, reduction of waste, Lead Times, increased flexibility, etc.

In conclusion, it is worth underlining two aspects which are fundamental if Westerners are going to understand the logic of MBP. They are similar to the factors dealt with in Chapter 6. The first aspect concerns a limit of three priorities per year. This is a strictly entrepreneurial logic (an entrepreneur is a person who can identify and concentrate on the priorities of the moment). It presupposes the fact that the smaller the number of objectives (ideally only one), the more management will be effective. These objectives are constantly monitored through "visual control" and pursued day by day.

This means that instead of planning, for example, ten objectives with 5–10% improvements each, it is better and more effective to tackle one or two at a time, with improvement objectives of at least 30%. It is then possible to concentrate on these, examining them and studying improvement actions with suitable deployment, without being distracted by other objectives. Management of such objectives through visual control of suitable operating performance indicators makes it possible to abandon the ineffective and frustrating practice of evaluating progress on the basis of monthly reports – usually too late to take action if problems occur, or to seize opportunities which have arisen in the meantime.

The second aspect concerns the importance of "how". On the one hand, "how much" (the numerical result) is usually very important for that year's business plan while, on the other hand, the "how" is very important for the "health" of the company (its results in future years). As we know, Total Quality places great emphasis on the second aspect and, therefore, MBP emphasizes the "how". For example, if the objective were to reduce the cost by 10% of purchased materials, MBO would limit itself to requesting "numerical" contributions from all the managers – leaving them to define the "how". The result could be to achieve the numerical objective planned for the year and save the business plan, but at a cost of putting the suppliers into considerable difficulty. It would probably be tackled through making impositions on suppliers or through reducing the quality of the supplies. This would be paid for a few years later when the company would find itself with suppliers "squeezed dry" and not up to the standard of the competition. MBP requires that "how" annual objectives are achieved should be planned and pursued with the aim of not weakening, but preferably improving the business factors important for the future (the "company health" factors).

In the supplies example, the "how" could be identified within the logic of Comakership (increase of volumes for each supplier, evaluations by total costs and not by price, elimination or reduction of inspection costs, etc.). What is important is that the "how" should systematically be an issue for everyone. Coherence of action is often more important than its detailed content.

MANAGEMENT BY PROCESSES*

While Management by Policy is the natural evolution of Effective Management, the natural evolution of BPR is Management by Processes, which enables the "by processes" approach to be transformed into a routine, management mechanism. At the same time it provides a continuous improvement activity for the company.

This management mechanism has been developed in the configuration presented here, by leading Western companies, generally within the scope of Total Quality approaches (although not always). It has no corresponding mechanism in the orthodox Japanese Total Quality model, where Cross-Functional Management is applied. The differences are not striking but they exist and are due to the greater need to emphasize the "process" dimension in the West as it was not recognized at a management level here.

With Management by Processes it is possible to operate in such a way that the interfunctional activities prevail over the functions, independently of the organizational structure already existing. This provides the correct supervision and improvement of company processes in daily work. The instrument enables us to identify the processes on which to intervene and operate in a structured way, and to improve them, without modifying the company organization chart. The only (important) organizational variation is the creation of Process Owners, those responsible for the processes.

Management by Processes can be activated downstream to a BPR intervention or as a new operative method, starting from the existing situation (Figure 7.5). This paragraph describes both these possibilities. The rationale on which Management by Processes is based is the same as the "by process" approach and therefore the same as BPR. However some principles have greater operative importance. They are:

- Focusing on the processes seen as supplier–customer chains
- Continuous alignment with internal clients' (and external customers') needs

---

* This section written in collaboration with Marco Biroli, Galgano & Associates.

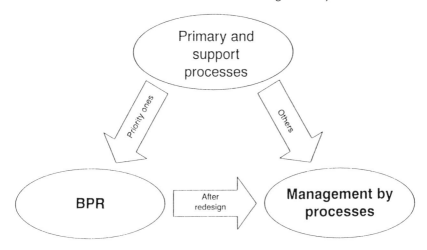

Figure 7.5   *Management by Processes and Business Process Reengineering.*

- The need to keep under control the process performances and the utilized procedures
- Improvement activities guided by priority policies.

This last principle is the departure point from which to start Managing by Processes. If we really want to improve the company's general results we must choose which of its processes to act on with priority. Then we must decide which changes to make in the chosen processes, make them and lastly, manage them correctly to maintain over time the performances thus achieved. These are the three stages shown in Figure 7.6. It is a continuous cycle that produces, with time, improvements in all the company processes. If unsatisfactory performances have already been identified, the self assessment stage can be passed over. In such a situation the choice of process occurs by necessity or opportunity, the objective being to solve the problem that already exists.

The First Stage: Identifying the Priority Processes

Clearly the choice of processes on which to intervene must be closely connected to the strategic objectives the company intends to pursue, and to the performances the existing processes obtain, particularly in reference to the competition. The

The three key moments

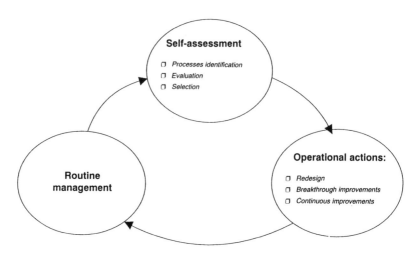

Figure 7.6   *Management by Processes approach.*

top management is asked to choose two to three processes on which to concentrate effort, time and resources. The method normally used requires some operative stages (Figure 7.7). The first is identifying and describing the short- to medium-term strategic objectives. Examples of strategic objectives are: increasing market share; improving internal efficiency; improving contacts with key customers; improving the effectiveness and speed of communications (both internal and external). Subsequently the management must find the key success factors, which are those internal factors through which the strategic objectives can be pursued. Here are some examples of key factors: quality, time, costs, service, order traceability, respecting commitments with customers, technical support, knowing the market, Lead Time, active commitment to product quality.

Choosing the key factors is always a delicate stage for the choice of the priority processes and requires the following clarifications:

- The number must be limited (from about four for a company already in a critical situation, where a maximum concentration of effort is required, up to a maximum of eight in more favourable situations).

The operational steps

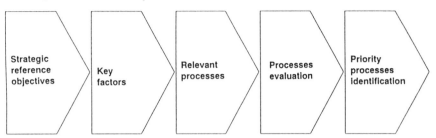

Figure 7.7   *Self-assessment.*

- The key factors need the consensus of all the participants. It is certainly not expedient to make decisions on a majority vote because whoever disagrees is unlikely to be active in defining and implementing changes, and might even create obstacles.
- Not all the key factors have the same weight because they are tied to the external market situation and the competition. It is therefore necessary to establish different weights (in percentage form, for instance). A helpful contribution in defining these weights comes from customer satisfaction analyses and Benchmarking.

At this point we must find the internal processes related to the key factors, the processes that have a significant impact on their achievement. This can be done in two ways:

1   By making a list of all the internal processes
2   By identifying which processes are related to each key factor

The same hierarchical level must be employed for the definition of the processes so as not to put macro-processes in together with others of more limited interest. The following is a list of the processes identified by a commercial company:

- Managing proposal
- Managing orders
- Supplying materials
- Managing returns
- Distributing the goods

- Monitoring the orders
- Informing customers
- Visiting customers
- Gathering information from the market
- Identifying products
- Developing a project
- Demonstrating products
- Informing the factories on quality requirements
- Informing the factories on noncompliance
- Identifying financial trends
- Implementing innovations into the service

At this point a matrix is prepared that links the processes with the key factors. The priority processes can be defined from this. Judgement will take into account the impact a process has on company business (B) and the current Quality level of the processes (Q). Matching impact on Business against performance Quality enables us to identify which are the priority processes. Identification is obtained by putting the pairs of values obtained in a "B–Q" Matrix (Figure 7.8). In this way a critical area will be put in evidence, indicating the processes which have a high impact on Business and are executed with insufficient quality. The area can be seen in the upper left hand corner of the figure. These are the processes that need priority intervention.

The Second Stage: The Operative Activities

Once the priority processes have been decided, the improvement process must be activated. I suggest an approach divided into the sequential stages shown in Figure 7.9.

The first stage is an analysis of the existing situation. This helps to identify clearly the aims of the process and the connections between it and the outside world and with the other activities of the company. This is the point at which a person is appointed to be responsible for the process, the Process Owner. The choice of Process Owner is fundamentally important for the success of the project. He or she is responsible both for the improvement phase and for the continuous supervision of per-

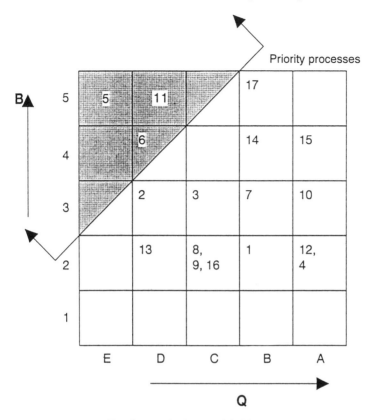

B = Impact on Business (1 low, 5 high)

Q = Quality of Performance (E low, A high)

Figure 7.8   *B–Q Matrix.*

formance. In the first place the Process Owner sets up a multi-functional work group which analyzes the process, identifies the possibilities of improvement and the ways to intervene on it, carries out modifications and checks the results. The Process Owner becomes the real manager of the process and is responsible for achieving the objectives. He or she examines all the operative stages to seek out the bottlenecks and problems and agrees on the improvement actions with those responsible for the functions. He or she must therefore have the indisputable leadership

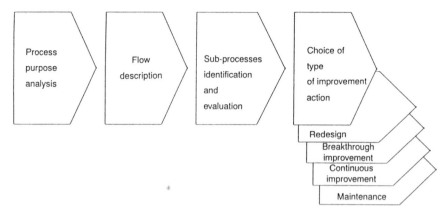

Figure 7.9   *Operational steps.*

that comes from competence (to ignore this factor would be a passport to failure) and possess excellent relational capacities. He or she is normally chosen by the top management team that has decided on the processes to improve. It is indispensable that the person be officially entrusted with total responsibility for the process. This will give the Process Owner the status necessary to enable him or her to operate. The rewarding mechanisms must also be adapted to ensure that the role is fulfilled effectively. They must be linked to the achievement of the global results of the process.

The identification of the purposes of the process is followed by the definition of its mission (the very reason for its existence). "Complaints management", for example, has the following missions: solving customers' problems, reducing loss of public image for the company, and gathering information to improve the product and service. Defining the missions of a process formally is not a trivial matter. It puts into evidence right from the beginning exactly what objectives the process must pursue. In other words, it emphasizes the value the process generates for the customer.

The analysis proceeds with the definition of the limits of the process (where it begins and where it ends). Precise and identifiable events are defined (such as the emission of documents, traceable information) to provide a time reference, which is necessary if we want to measure the process Lead Time (which almost always happens). After this the suppliers are identified (persons/functions that provide products or services – inputs – used by the process) and the customers, who are all those who use the outputs produced by the process, inside or outside the company. Both the inputs and the outputs must be clearly identified and described. As we have seen, all processes have the primary objective of satisfying their customers. This is the concept of effectiveness. It is therefore essential to define most clearly what the elements that determine satisfaction are. This means knowing what customers' expectations are.

Until now the process has been analyzed by looking at it in relation to the outside world, without looking at it from the inside. However, to be able to improve it we must also know how the process is currently being executed. In fact (unlike BPR) Management by Processes begins with the existing situation, which must be clearly held in mind.

The current process must be rendered visible and this is done by describing its flow. There are various techniques in use to map processes. The most complete and widely-used method is the interfunctional flow diagram (Figure 7.10). This diagram immediately shows up the fragmentation of the flow and the presence of backward recycles. It facilitates identification of the activities with and those without added value. It is also relatively easy to design. Whichever technique is chosen, care must be taken to describe the process "as it really is today" and not as it should operate on the basis of the procedure that describes it. It is precisely from these differences that interesting points for improvement can emerge. In most cases, in fact, the official flow is often put aside in practice in the interests of speed and flexibility. One of the statements repeated most often during process analysis is: "If we followed the procedure we would be even more behind or worse."

Evaluating the Sub-processes

Not all the stages of a process have the same critical levels of effectiveness and efficiency. If we want to intervene with good results it is almost always necessary to divide the process into significant, homogeneous parts and then choose the most suitable form of action. The approach presented here uses a method

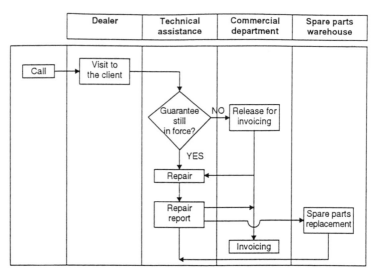

Figure 7.10   *Interfunctional flow design (technical assistance).*

similar to that seen in the self-diagnosis used to choose the critical processes. In this case the aim is the analysis of the sub-processes. The key factors become the elements that determine the success of the process. A matrix is prepared linking the sub-processes and the key factors (weighted if necessary), and the contribution of every sub-process to realizing the key factors is determined. By pairing these with an evaluation of the quality of the current performance, we can prepare the B–Q Matrix shown in Figure 7.11. This defines four zones which correspond to different types of intervention. We shall now analyze each of these zones in detail.

Zone 1 – Sub-processes Needing to be Redesigned

These are sub-processes with a high impact on the result and insufficient performance quality. They probably need drastic intervention, redesigning the process, creating a new flow and assigning different responsibilities. In this case we can go back and start from scratch, applying a similar approach to BPR, or we can apply the added-value analysis procedure. By examining the activities described in the flow diagram three types of activity can be identified:

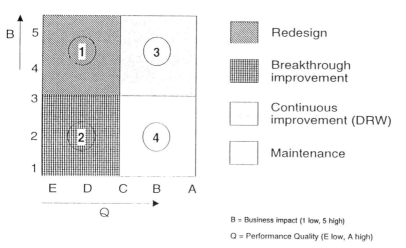

Figure 7.11   *Sub-processes: Choice of action type.*

1 *Activities with external added value.* These are activities that
   generate values perceived by outside customers. They are
   fundamentally important for customer satisfaction and must
   therefore be executed with the greatest quality possible. It
   must be made clear what needs the processes respond to and
   the necessary resources must be assigned to them and
   increased if required.

2 *Activities with internal added value.* These correspond to the
   requirements of the organization for the maintenance of control and the efficient execution of activities with added value
   for the final customer. They must be reduced to an absolute
   minimum and cost little or nothing.

3 *Activities with no added value.* These activities do not respond
   either to the needs of the outside customer or to those of an
   internal client. They are therefore wasteful and must be eliminated or at least drastically reduced.

The following are examples of activities of the last type: transport (of products or information), control (product testing,
checking and approving documents, designs, forms, etc.) and
stocking (of materials, documents, data). Waiting times are also
to be classified in this category. Sometimes strong resistance is

generated by the elimination of these activities. For example, the elimination of signatures of approval, which often have no added value, can require changes in delegation and the removal of the associated "power".

Redesigning a process usually requires the following type of intervention:

- Realignment between suppliers and customers
- Redefinition of roles/responsibilities
- Standardization
- Simplification/removal of bureaucracy
- Training
- Definition of process indicators
- Use of information technology (IT)

At this point we are ready to put the redesigned process into action. If possible, it is useful to make a small-scale test of the new flow so as to check its results and add any finishing touches to the design. Lastly, informing and training the people involved will be necessary steps to overcome the resistance to change that is typically the greatest difficulty in implementation.

Zone 2 – Sub-processes Requiring Breakthrough Improvements

These are sub-processes with significant impacts on the result, whose performances are unsatisfactory. They identify activities which do not necessarily need redesigning but must be drastically improved. The approach recommended in this case is the SEDAC method (described in Chapter 6), which uses visual systems for continuous monitoring of the performances to be improved (time, quality, costs). By wide staff involvement it enables the personnel to identify problems and find improvement solutions.

An example of the application of this procedure to the reduction of Lead Time is shown in the flow diagram + SEDAC in Figure 7.12. The current flow of the process is identified and put on the chart, describing the activities and connections in a manner simple and easy to understand. There will be two indicators: one shows the flow time, the other expresses the quality of the process. Both must be updated as often as possible and the chart

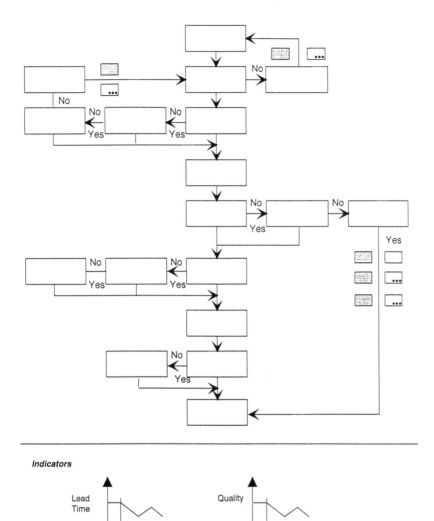

Figure 7.12 *Flow diagram + SEDAC (Flow–AC)*

must be put where everybody can see it. The SEDAC leader encourages everyone involved to write up on the cards the problems they meet with in practice at the various stages of the process and at the same time looks for ideas and suggestions to solve them. He or she concentrates everyone's attention on the problem examined, supervises it continuously and uses the experience of all the people concerned with the linear and rapid progression of the process, without the need to call meetings. The most interesting ideas are put into practice, and their effectiveness is shown by the indicators. The method is extremely effective and if well managed it can produce Lead Time improvements of 30–50% and/or quality improvement of 50–90% in just three to four months.

Zone 3 – Continuous Improvement

This area deals with the sub-processes that have great importance in pursuing the process objectives and that already give satisfactory performances. They must be followed with particular care so as to continue giving performances in alignment with requirements. Breakthroughs are not needed in these cases, just small steps and continual improvements. To this aim there is a specific methodology from Total Quality called DDM (see the following paragraph).

Zone 4 – Maintenance

The sub-processes in the lower right hand corner square are those that have only a slight impact on the process objectives and are executed with satisfactory quality. The action they require is simply the maintenance in time of the current performances and adjustment to customers' requests. The DDM approach just mentioned is the answer to these requirements but it is enough simply to apply it to the definition and monitoring stage (on outputs and process) without employing any resources in the search for improvements. On a practical level, the stages to follow are the same as in the preceding case.

DAY TO DAY MANAGEMENT

The essence of DDM, also called Quality in Daily Work (QIDW), is to focus company personnel on continuous improvement and the customer by activating internal vendor–vendee chains. What it achieves is the supervision and management of improvement in every routine corporate activity and process, with the aim of

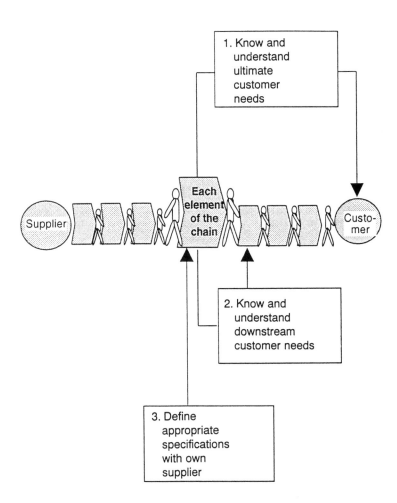

Figure 7.13   *Processes as supplier–customer chain.*

satisfying the final customer, as well as all internal customers. DDM is the mechanism which translates the concept of "market-in" into a practical organizational fact. The concept is illustrated in Figure 7.13. DDM is an organizational mechanism managed strictly by the line. The main sponsors, responsible for its management and improvement objectives, are the heads of each unit in the organization (office or department supervisor). In theory, DDM involves all personnel. All the organizational tools of Total Quality for developing improvements are used (Project Groups, Individual Tasks, CEDAC, etc.). The supervisors are trained in the most appropriate organizational tools and methodologies according to the type of improvement objective. The contribution of DDM to company improvement can be considered as follows: while MBP normally focuses on obtaining improvements greater than 30% of existing margins on priority objectives, DDM normally ensures a general improvement (at least 2–5% per annum) in all the routine processes. The differences between

	Management by Policies	Day to Day Management
Purpose	Drastic improvements (Breakthroughs)	Maintenance and improvement
Standards	Redesign	Followed and improved
Basic activities	Policy deployment	Process maintenance and standardization
Main process	Finding the right things to do	Doing things in the right way
Start-up and management	Top management	Each manager/unit
People involved in "plan"	From top to middle managers	Unit managers
People involved in "do"	Everybody who can contribute	Everybody

Figure 7.14   *MBP vs DDM.*

MBP and DDM in terms of results and organizational methods are summarized in Figure 7.14.

DDM (together with MBP) may be considered the crucial test of whether a company is really working within the rationale of Total Quality. It contains two ingredients which are fundamental to Total Quality: orientation to both outside customers and internal clients, and a continuous and organized bottom-up improvement activity.

In more technical terms the characteristics of DDM are as follows:

- It is applied at the micro-unit level (office, department) and is used in all the units of the company (generalized application)
- It is a permanent, continuous process, which is carried out on a daily basis
- It has the same continuity as the operating activities and processes of the unit
- It is applied to the normal routine activities of the unit
- It takes as its reference/objective the satisfaction of the customers of the unit (the next office/department downstream is the customer)
- It makes improvements through the management, control and improvement of the internal processes of the unit

The operating process through which this is achieved is summarized in Figure 7.15. When a company uses this mechanism in the context of a management system which already includes Management by Processes, a different DDM approach is followed. This is illustrated in Figure 7.16. The activities are as follows:

- Each office lists the activities carried out
- It links them to the business processes which pass through them, collating them in a coherent manner
- It identifies the related outputs (also collated by process)
- It "isolates" the activities not directly linked to the business processes (for a later analysis of their usefulness)
- It identifies the internal customers for whom its outputs are intended

- It interviews these customers to identify their needs, the critical issues related to their own outputs, the most appropriate performance indicators, and the possibilities of increasing their satisfaction
- It analyzes its own processes and reviews them with its suppliers, in order to identify opportunities for improvement

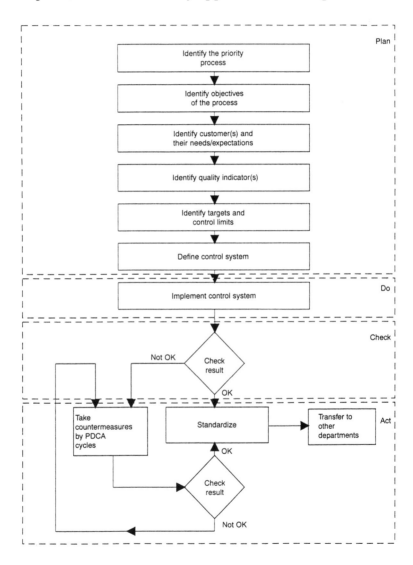

Figure 7.15 *Continuous improvement process of DDM.*

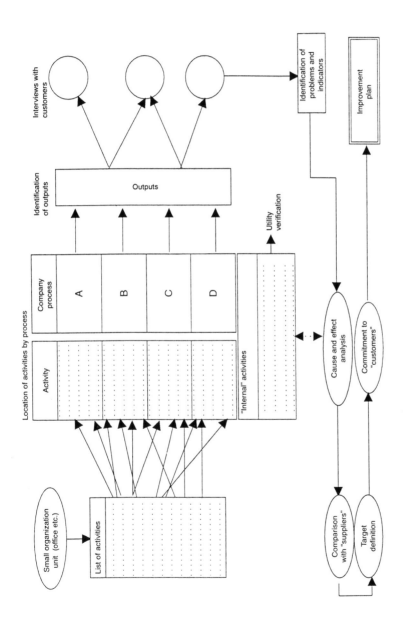

Figure 7.16   *DDM in Management by Process environment.*

- It chooses priorities and agrees improvement objectives with its customers
- It defines the methods for carrying out the improvement activity
- It prepares improvement plans
- It monitors the processes/activities involved
- It achieves the improvement
- It carries on to define further objectives

8
How to choose a development path

It sometimes seems today that a host of management magazines, books, consultants and conferences all bombard us with a tidal wave of new approaches and new acronyms. While this may be a positive thing because it means we are continually receiving new stimuli to look for opportunities for improvement, there are some hidden dangers in the situation. The first is due to the fact that not all of these new approaches are really new. Sometimes it is know-how that is already known, simply recycled under another label.

The second danger is the disorientation effect – faced with all these stimuli we just don't know which way to turn. If we are unlucky enough to come up against the situation described, where there is actually nothing new in a newly presented approach, our disorientation turns to rejection. Naturally, we promise ourselves, we will never rise to the bait again! This means, however, that we risk losing the good part, the "substantially" new, together with the bad.

A third danger comes from the fact that we lack a reference model to help us understand how all these approaches are linked together. The risk here is to find ourselves making parallel reorganizations without realizing the synergies, or even managing projects that are actually in contradiction with one another. Unfortunately this danger is congenital with the (otherwise professionally justified) existence of business consultancy firms which are specialized only in certain specific approaches. In fact their objective is to sell their own approach without embarking on more complex adventures which may not be easy to manage for those who are only armed with specialized know-how. This is due to the following reasons:

1   Real management consultants are hard to come by, both because it is not an easy job and because their value is not always rewarded economically.
2   High level consultants from the large international consulting firms tend to be oriented towards the strategic aspects and/or sales rather than operative assistance.
3   Management consultants working with small to medium companies, and freelance consultants tend to remain outside the international circle of the best practice companies. They therefore have rather limited horizons, partly because they cannot invest enough in that direction, given the dimensions of their activities.
4   It is easier to find good consultants specialized in particular approaches. However, they must be kept within their own fields or they can create problems as they tend to relate every problem to their own specializations or solutions.
5   Lastly, it often happens that consultants simply transform an innovative approach into the sale of information systems supporting their approach.

This is one of the easiest business approaches for the large consultancy firms. The case of Business Process Reengineering (BPR) is typical: a reorganizational project can easily reach the ratio of 1:10 to 1:100 with an information system (every day of reorganizational consultancy is sold together with 10 to 100 days of information consultancy and installation). This does not mean that information systems are unnecessary. It simply means that the consultant's interest tends to be aimed at the applications he or she feels most at ease with or which are more economically interesting for him or her.

How can these dangers be avoided? There can be no doubt that the increased complexity of the consultancy services and approaches available means that company managers must improve their capacity to deal with them. It is a vicious circle:

- The most advanced/complex companies require consultancy services that are increasingly complex and specialized (handled by highly capable managers)
- The approaches become increasingly refined and specialized
- So do the consultants
- Middle level managers must inescapably become more and more informed and able to understand the approaches

In this chapter I will try to give a contribution to overcome this situation by fitting the most recent management approaches into a reference model. I will deal only with the organizational and management aspects of the question. The three most widely mentioned approaches today are:

1 Total Quality
2 Breakthrough
3 Management by Process (and/or BPR)

By applying the considerations I have made so far I will give an idea of how they are related. I will therefore first summarize the general rationale of each approach and then concentrate on the relationships. The reference scheme is shown in Figure 8.1.

THE TOTAL QUALITY APPROACH

From the standpoint of organization and management, the Total Quality system can be summed up in the mechanisms I will describe now (for greater details see Chapter 7).

On the planning level, the Total Quality rationale uses part of the Management by Policies cycle, identified as "definition of the annual policies". This stage is developed on the basis of two fundamental sources of information: the largest problems of the preceding year and the long-term policies. These are planning policies that we in the West have chosen to call "visions", while the Japanese refer to them as "long-term policies". The main output of Total Quality planning is, in the end, the definition of the "policy for the year", which we often prefer to call "priority of the year" in the West. It may therefore be concluded that on a

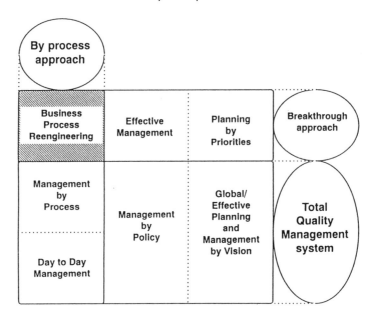

Figure 8.1   *Possible approaches.*

business planning level Total Quality adopts an approach that we could define Planning by Visions and by Priority.

On an operative level Total Quality has three management dimensions:

1   Management by Policy that manages the activities related to the policy/priority of the year
2   Managing by Process (or Cross-Functional Management), that aims at improving the business processes and interfunctional matters (improvement in organization)
3   Day to Day Management that guarantees continuous improvement in the supplier-to-internal client system (along the operative processes)

THE BREAKTHROUGH APPROACH

On a planning level this approach concentrates on the identification of the priority levers by which to pursue the chosen objective. It could be called Planning by Priorities.

On an operative level, as seen in Chapter 1, the Breakthrough approach includes two types of action:

1 Actions by the line management by adopting Effective Management (a system of special Management of Priorities)
2 Reorganizational projects through the BPR approach (redesigning the organization)

THE "BY PROCESS" APPROACH

This approach has not been presented in detail so far in this book. It unites all the organizational and managerial aspects coming under the process rationale. For the organizational aspects it uses BPR, and for the operational aspects both Management by Process (for management responsibilities) and Day to Day Management (to manage the continuous improvement stage).

After this brief description of the three approaches (Total Quality, Breakthrough, Processes) I can make some considerations which I shall divide into "technical" considerations and "approach/path" considerations.

TECHNICAL CONSIDERATIONS

The Breakthrough approach, as mentioned in Chapter 1, constitutes in practice also a way of activating the management mechanisms of Total Quality through its by-products. Effective Management, for instance, is a simplified version of Management by Policy. When a company that has successfully applied Effective Management wants to adopt the method systematically to tackle all the Breakthrough objectives that can be managed on the line, the organizational response is to activate the Management by Policy mechanism.

However, this consideration is reductive because it is also possible to take an almost opposite direction. Quite often a company already in Management by Policy decides to activate special management that is particularly effective for its most challenging objectives. It will be at this point that it finds the Effective Management mechanisms responding to its requirements. It can then be used as the operative dimension for its most important objectives and grafted onto the normal base of Management by Policy. This is the case, for example, of companies as SGS-THOMPSON and ALLIED SIGNAL.

This is also true for Planning by priorities, which is the precursor of Planning by Vision and by Policy but at the same time can be used specifically for the more demanding objectives. The same applies to BPR which activates Management by Process as its natural outcome, but it is still periodically used to redesign the most critical processes of the moment.

Examining the coherent aspects from the "by process" standpoint, the logical deduction at this point is that BPR, besides naturally activating Management by Process, can also easily activate Effective Management approaches for those objectives that can/must be pursued by the line management. Naturally it must first go through a phase of Planning by Priorities.

The natural operative application of Management by Process is Day to Day Management. With its continuous bottom-up improvement rationale, Day to Day Management is the most culturally suitable way to enter more deeply into the world of Total Quality, which in its turn will inevitably activate Management by Policy.

APPROACH/PATH CONSIDERATIONS

The technical paths have been illustrated. It will now be interesting to take a look at the rationale of the initial approaches, or how to enter the world of innovative approaches. My view of this aspect is very pragmatic: you enter by exploiting your existing energies. By this I mean it is much easier to activate new management methods by making the best use of the energies and drive already present in the company than by trying to persuade all the executive staff how excellent a new approach is. New methods must be conveyed and activated through something concrete that is already felt as important by the management. Only after having success with a special approach can we talk about adopting the new methods systematically. The energies I refer to are generally connected to existing needs or objectives that are not being solved easily with the methods already in practice. In this sort of situation new methodological help is well accepted.

The variety of approaches suggested can be reduced to a few basic types. If the existing need is of the type "obtain a drastic operative improvement", the most suitable "way in" is obviously Effective Management. In this case, however, it should not be presented as a mechanism but simply as an *ad hoc* methodology. It will be explained step by step, following the system of the levers/actions identified to pursue the objective. Once success has been reached, the decision to adopt the method permanently will follow logically and the company will be well on the way to the Management by Policy rationale and ready to try out equally effective methodologies on organizational objectives as well. Objectives requiring reorganizations mean adopting BPR. Again, it will be proposed as an *ad hoc* methodology and only after the initial success will the company proceed to adopt Management by Process and/or Effective Management, and so on.

If the existing energies in a company are on a more "noble" plane, oriented to activating new organizational and managerial methods, the entrance suggested is the "by process" approach in its entirety, or it may even be Total Quality – if there are strong enough cultural energies present. We have seen then that every way in is good conceptually, but we cannot say the same in practice. We need to use the best "entrance" for the company's immediate needs. This is the only way to gain an adequate commitment by managers, otherwise the urgent problems will take the upper hand over the merely important. Despite all their good intentions, the managers will never be able to overcome the pressing needs of the short term to achieve what they think is "simply" good but not urgent.

It will be helpful to go into further detail about a situation that is very frequently found in companies nowadays. Supposing a company has attempted methodological experiments in Total Quality. It can find itself in one of two opposing situations:

1   It does not know how to transform a successful, but experimental, Total Quality programme into a new way of managing the company

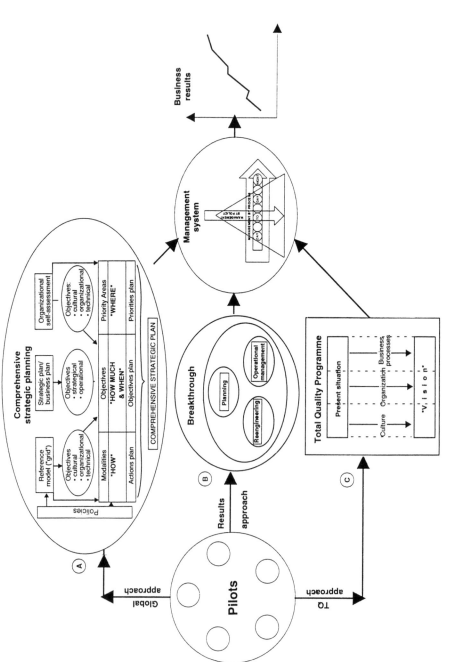

Figure 8.2 *Development of the business management approach (through Total Quality).*

2   It is trying to see if Total Quality is really effective after experiments that have not been entirely satisfactory

In this case the possible paths suggested are shown in Figure 8.2. The starting point is the existence of some pilot Total Quality experiences. In such a situation three different types of situation/energies can occur, with three corresponding different paths. Situation A may be synthesized as follows:

- "We are very satisfied with the outcome of the experiments"
- "We realize there is great potential in the possibility of managing the company differently"
- "We have decided to adopt systematically the new global/entrepreneurial management method"

This is obviously the case with most potential. The energy catalyzed is of the global/entrepreneurial type. The path suggested (path A) will enable the company to focus rapidly on the new management methods of the business, which may be summed up in the following way:

1   Focus:
   - Development of a global entrepreneurial management system
2   Advantages:
   - Guaranteed results both in the short and long term
   - Managerial and organizational improvements at all levels
3   Disadvantages:
   - Complexity of the approach
   - Need for high commitment and supervision levels

Situation B may be expressed in the following ways:

1   First alternative:
   - "We are very satisfied/surprised with the results obtained"
   - "We would like to apply these approaches to something more important"

- "Please don't talk about philosophy and culture, only concrete facts and results; we can't take the rest very seriously"
2 Second alternative:
  - "We are not at all satisfied with the results obtained"
  - "Results fairly satisfying, you may proceed, but we of the top management must deal with more important things"

The energy catalyzed in these cases is oriented towards operative results. In both cases the B path is suggested, which focuses on important short-term results. It may be described as follows:

1 Focus:
  - Adoption of approaches strongly oriented to the result
2 Advantages:
  - Ease of short-term results
  - Strong demonstrative effect
  - Ease/speed of application
3 Disadvantages:
  - The evolutionary process is not activated automatically
  - The Total Quality approach is not made evident in the short term

Situation C reference convictions may be expressed as follows:

- "Very interesting experience"
- "We realize it is first of all a problem of cultural and organizational evolution"
- "We believe in the Total Quality approach and we know the results will only be the natural consequences of the application of this strategy"

The energy catalyzed is strongly oriented towards values and human resources. In this case path C is suggested. It is the "pure" path of Total Quality, that plans and creates cultural/organizational evolutions towards a Vision. Path C is as follows:

1 Focus:
  - Development of a global Total Quality programme
2 Advantages:
  - Coherent and continuous development of the company

- Cultural and management improvement at all levels
3 Disadvantages:
  - Limited orientation to Breakthrough results
  - Little concrete results in the short term

Naturally the goal of all three pathways is practically the same, to guarantee for the company the capacity to achieve important global results. While it is perhaps true that the cultural orientation will always remain a little apart, it is also true that in each of the three cases the companies will find themselves, at the end of their path, with very similar managerial methods: the trio of Management by Policy, Management by Process and Continuous Improvement Management. They may be called by different names and their proportion in the management mix may differ, but there can be no doubt that a company capable of important results cannot do without these three operative dimensions. An interpretive map of the dimensions and operative methods for improvement in a company is shown in Figure 8.3. (mainly for the experts of Total Quality).

		Level of action		
		Operational	Organizational	Strategic
Improvement Amount	Kaizen	(Bottom-up improvement) ⊓ Day to Day Management (Kaizen)	(Systematic improvement) ⊓ Internal vendor-vendee chains ⊓ Q, C, D Campaigns	(Systematic improvement as strategic factor) ⊓ Managing by Policy organization ⊓ Human resources empowerement (as strategic lever)
	Breakthrough	(Operational Breakthroughs) ⊓ Magagement by Priority (Effective / Focused Management)	(Organizational Breakthroughs) ⊓ Business Processes Reengineering/ Restructuring	(Strategic Breakthroughs) ⊓ Changes in strategies ⊓ Changes in planning methods

Figure 8.3 *Improvement approaches.*

9
Beyond Business Process Reengineering

ORGANIZATION BY PROCESSES

Once a company has consolidated its management capability in the two operative areas, Management by Process and Day to Day Management, it is technically ready to modify its organization as well. It will then be in a position to exploit all the potential that the "by process" approach can offer. As you may have noticed, I said that organization by process can be put into practice "once" the management mechanisms have been put into practice. We often come across companies who set themselves objectives that modify their structures and organizations right from the early stages of the "by process" approach. This is decidedly out of place, even dangerous, because the mechanisms I have illustrated so far do not require modifications to the structure. They can work perfectly well with the same existing organization. Their "institutional" purpose is simply to transmit to the managerial line, by suitable mechanisms, the responsibility and the capability to improve the company's business processes. It may be said that, within a Total Quality framework, they make it possible to transform into practice the concept that organizational improvement must be managed by the line and not by the organization department. The task of the organization department is to give the OK to proposed and activated modifications, after checking that there is no danger of compromising the balance of the firm as a whole and that the modifications are not incoherent with other procedures and processes. The principle put into practice is that the procedures (that are "the best way found so far to carry out the relative processes") are now supervised and continuously improved by the managerial line itself. It is dangerous because it could trigger problem-raising modifications to responsibility attribution, creating unwanted overlapping. It is quite common nowadays in companies to mistake process responsibility for that of the individual results of the business activities that use the process. In other cases process responsibility is also activated on the business results, adding it to function responsibilty and the transversal product or business responsibility, in a matrix format. And to think that the "by processes" organization is a perfect way to overcome the difficulties in co-responsibility at the cross points of matrix strutures!

This certainly does not mean that co-responsibility is abolished. It will be assumed by groups, aligned along the operative processes and not crossing over on two or more perpendicular responsibilities. The "by process" organization is none other than a form of lean organization. In its most advanced configuration it can be achieved with just three areas of responsibility, each of which is independently operative:

1   Business/results responsibilities
2   Organizational responsibilities
3   Functional responsibilities

It is this separation that gives a really lean structure, divided into a limited number of positions and managerial levels. The structure is determined entirely by the business responsibilities, which become decidedly simplified – and more focused – thanks to the transposition of the other two areas. There will be, of course, a widening of the "span of control" and therefore of the number of hierarchical references. This is a typical situation in lean structures. The resulting operative configuration is described below.

Business/Results Responsibilities

These belong to the operative line management that manages activities bearing directly on the business results. These responsibilities generally coincide with activities that are carried on within the primary processes and form the only real managerial line. They are usually articulated by product line (or some other form of stratification) and deal, for example, with product development, sales, and so on. These are the positions that are responsible for the operative results and form the supervising and management structure of the annual economic results.

An example of such an organization in a "production to order" company is shown in Figure 9.1. Notice how the classical intermediate figures of sales manager, production manager and works manager are eliminated. They become pure functional responsibilities (as we shall see later) with no direct contribution to the business activities flow.

The Organizational Responsibilities

These are the new responsibilities introduced with the "by process" approach. Like the preceding type, they are also matrix responsibilities, but they are on the organizing level. There is no direct co-responsibility for the business results.

These people, the Process Owners, are responsible for supervising and improving the operating processes. The extent of necessary improvement is established annually, it may depend on the planning period involved, or it may be decided for exceptional cases when necessary. Thus they take on responsibilities once borne by the organizational department/service. The processes supervised/improved by the Process Owners can be primary (sales, purchasing, designing, supply chain) or support processes (budgeting, planning, and so on). Objectives and results are usually expressed in terms of quality, time and process costs. It is in this area that the future competitive capabilities of the company are at stake. In fact the processes are used by the people responsible for company business for their activities and objectives. The Process Owners respond to the general management but not so frequently as the business area (every six months/year rather than daily/weekly/monthly).

The Functional Responsibilities

Those with such responsibilities have a traditional title but their task changes radically. They no longer have direct business

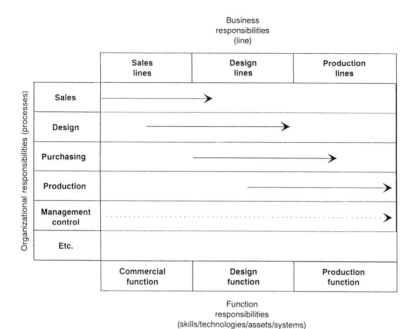

Figure 9.1   *Example of a "three dimension" matrix organization.*

responsibility as they must only respond for the capacities of the resources supervised by their function (in terms of people, technologies and systems). The need to improve these capacities is, of course, identified at the same time as the need to improve the processes. They are matrix responsibilities, like the previous two, but they operate on another level, that of the capabilities of people and technologies and their periodic assignment to the business lines. So they, too, are in indirect co-responsibility, having no specific business objectives.

The Operative Model

The three areas of responsibility, as we have seen, are matrix-integrated. This, however, takes place on different planes, meaning that the nature of the objectives assigned to each is different, so no direct or overlapping co-responsibilities for results can exist. Such co-responsibilities are found among the operatives, who are those responsible for the line and the people who physically carry out the company processes (who are responsible for business/results). The resulting structure has three dimensions (see Figure 9.1).

An example of an organization chart constructed along these lines is shown in Figure 9.2. It represents a customized product company with approximately 900 people on its payroll. As can be seen it is a very lean organization. There is a maximum of three hierarchical levels (following the production line), and span of control is very ample (no less than 15 positions report to the general manager). The number of operative/managerial positions is relatively limited (five report lines, the product lines and manufacturing lines).

To help understand the operative functioning of this organization, we could take the analogy of a transport business in a motorway's network. In such an example the business results are represented by the amount of transportations carried out. The processes are the motorways. The Process Owners are the people who must continuously maintain and improve them (by constructing better intersections connecting up with other motorways/processes, or raising the amount of sustainable traffic by adding another traffic lane, for instance, or by improving the quality of the surface, and so on). The functions represent the people whose task it is to supply the technical means to carry out the work: vehicles, service areas, drivers, fuel, and so on. They are responsible for supervision and for developing suitable resources, both human and technical, to enable the drivers to use the motorways (the business channels) in the most effective and efficient way. The people working on the functions must therefore know all the rules of the game, they must be trained, and they must know how to use new technologies when necessary (e.g. computer aided cruise on the vehicles). They must also know how to achieve different processes/speeds when the process is reengineered later. In other words the resources must be ready in quantity and quality to do the work as set out.

Business results are entirely in the hands of the drivers, or those who develop the path/transport. They can work both singly and in groups. For example, they can work in shifts, one

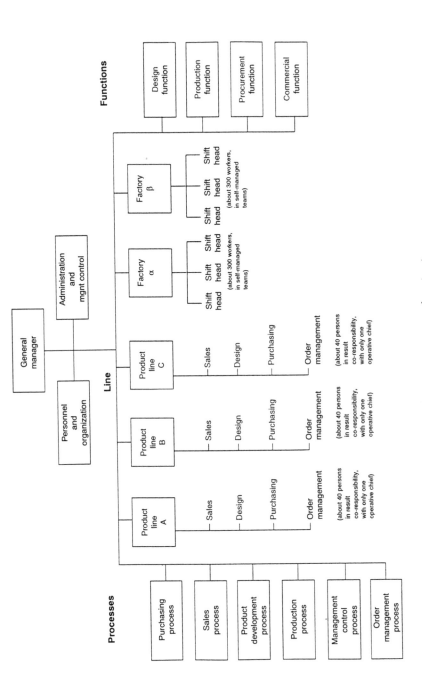

Figure 9.2 *Example of a matrix lean organization (business, processes, functions).*

after the other along the route, so they are all co-responsible for the global transport result. Applying our example to the company situation, this means there will be a driver for the first path (sales), a second one for the design stage, a third for the production stage, and so on. Each of them is concerned, of course, to make the transport works properly, so each one will try to make up for time lost in preceding stages or will work beyond his or her functional limits when necessary, in the effort to achieve the results.

The managing director will have frequent contact with the line (the drivers), probably via radio (that is in real time if necessary), to help them in the processes. He or she will be informed of the final results by the management control and will not need to contact either the function heads (responsible for the vehicles) systematically during current operative management or the Process Owners (responsible for the roadways). He or she will do so only on exceptional occasions, when it is found that they are not adequately serving those who carry out the work operatively. He or she will meet the latter something like once a month to maintain control of the situation. In this way we can see how the principle is applied that those who condition all a company's activities are those who generate value, those who use the primary processes. These are prepared by the Process Owners and are carried out by adequate human and technical resources (directly or in support) prepared and supplied by the function heads. Figure 9.3 shows a summary scheme of these types of responsibility.

A last example of the functioning of this organization can be made through the point of view of the human resources (the central operative figures). We'll take the example of a buyer. In the first place he or she will be prepared and updated by the head of the buying function to offer the performances required by the supplies process method, at the level planned for the next period by the Process Owner (for example, the buyer will know how to evaluate purchases "at total costs" rather than in the traditional way). At the beginning of the year or planning period, or at any other time necessary, the buyer will be assigned either temporarily or permanently, to a product line by the management committee. There he or she

	Business results	Human and technical resources	Organization (processes)
Line	Direct responsibility (co-responsibility/ along the process)	Utilization	Utilization
Process owner	Indirect co-responsibility (process capability)	Definition of best utilization standards	Set-up, supervision continuous improvement
Function responsibility	Indirect co-responsibility (resource capability)	Specific performance capabilities	Resource improvement

Figure 9.3   *Types of responsibility.*

will work on the business of the product line with other resources of other functions, under the coordination of the line/business head. As the buyer is linked to other people by objectives/results, he or she will often find himself having to intervene upstream or downstream, beyond his or her natural boundaries, in order to make the total process advance well. He or she will often have to make a direct contribution on the bottle-necks in the total process (for example by helping on the planning or engineering phases, if they become swamped at any time).

These examples give a clear idea of how these methods can help to overcome age-old problems of organization by creating an organizing structure that may seem complex on paper but is very simple in practice. The problems thus solved concern:

• The need for numerous hierarchical levels due to the fact that functions and results are supervised by the same structure. With the new system the function is separated.

- The need for large organization departments that improve the processes from outside, not wanting or being able to use the line for this. With the new system this is the task of the Process Owners.
- The difficulties in managing crossed objective co-responsibilities between functions and transversal activities, typical of traditional matrix structures, where interests are inevitably at cross purposes. With the new system, cross-objectives do not exist.
- The difficulties in setting up self-adapting and market-driven structures on the basis of actual needs and opportunities of the moment. With the new system, processes are "available" to be used according to the needs of the moment and are continuously adapted by the Process Owners when they are badly used or not used at all.
- The problem of managing the ambiguity of global responsibilities at the function chief or service head level, which have little contact with operations. It is far easier to manage such co-responsibilities and ambiguities at the operator level along the process, thanks to the concrete importance the factors determining results have for them.
- The difficulties in managing resource and career development by function channels. Job rotation and changing responsibilities become normal events with the new organization.

Notice how the rationale proposed causes a progressive shift of management methods towards "project" types, away from routine and functional rationales. The methods put forward by Tom Peters in his book *Liberation Management** are achieved this way as well.

There is another consideration, perhaps a little provoking, in favour of the new approaches. How much added value did a sales manager or a works manager place in the operational line produce? Probably much less than the damage caused by the slowing down of management due to his or her operational filter both downwards and upwards. How much was this due to the results of his or her sales force or production workers if not the

---

* Tom Peters, *Liberation Management*, Macmillan, London 1992.

algebraic sum of them all? It would be far better to use his or her abilities as a sales coach (as head of the function, no longer in the line) or as responsible for improving the sales process (as a Process Owner either permanently or temporarily).

Lastly, notice how many new and better chances for growth of staff are created by giving them the possibility to rotate over various line positions (orientation to business), Process Owner positions (organization orientation) and function leader positions (orientation to specialization). Yet widespread experimentation is still lacking. The few cases so far carried out cannot provide any guarantee of this, although they do indeed give good indications.

THE VIRTUAL-HOLONIC COMPANY

In the near future Business Process Reengineering (BPR) and Management by Processes will, paradoxically, be considered necessary but not enough by the very reasoning that is making them successful today. If, on the one hand, business processes cannot be improved by taking them from the functional angle alone, it is just as limiting to attempt to improve them only from a company angle, without a vision of the whole business process. It is important to recognize that today a company normally produces a maximum of 30–50% of its turnover internally and that this in turn is only a small percentage of the total value chain developed by the whole business process in which the company participates. Improving one's own business process simply on a company basis can therefore be dangerous. There is the risk of concentrating on a segment with a low value in the global economy of the whole process, or on a vulnerable segment. To appreciate which are the least vulnerable and highest value-added segments (the most important), it is necessary to have an overall vision of the whole value chain. This is the only way to realize one's own distinctive competences, how they can be best exploited and how best to modify them to become more competitive.

The best BPR aims to design and/or set up business process segments within a wider framework, which we must try to become aware of (at least passively, or better pro-actively). This sort of reasoning belongs to the virtual company, that is companies which put themselves together each time there appears the need or opportunity, in a rationale of open systems in different business sectors.

What is all this about? Let us see.*

The Scenario

The most forward-looking people in Japan and the USA (coordinated by state departments such as the US Ministry of Defense and the Japanese MITI) are studying a new business strategy to be diffused before the end of the century. These new approaches use definitions like "distributed autonomous production", "agile manufacturing", "open system enterprise", "pro-sumers", "plug companies", but I think the best definition of what is about to happen is "virtual-holonic enterprise". These models are based on structures made up of networks of small companies and operative units, physically distributed over large areas, which are simultaneously capable both of working in entrepreneurial autonomy and integrating with other companies. This model, for example, will enable small companies to operate in a new global context by activating large virtual enterprises that are able to compete with the great multinational enterprises. These possibilities are offered by the holonic system. Considering the current trends it looks as though this type of configuration will be quite a normal thing in the next century. These expectations are based on the following considerations.

When people started tilling the land most of the population consumed what it produced. What was not self-produced was furnished by craftspeople with whom the consumer interacted directly to obtain what he or she needed. Now, in the industrial age, we consume what others produce. In the future post-industrial age the producer and the consumer will come into direct contact once again (sometimes even physically), creating a closer, more direct form of communication. The consumer will intervene directly in the productive processes of his or her suppliers, conditioning them according to his or her own specific

---

* Extract from G. Merli and C. Saccani, *L'azienda olonico-virtuale*, Il Sole 24 Ore Libri, Milan 1994.

needs. This type of customer will be called a "pro-sumer" instead of a consumer.

The consumer's participation in production is an evolution of the concept of "service". The signs of developments now in use are getting stronger and coming from all directions. The need to rethink industrial production is felt by many, together with the need to introduce new organizing methods to respond to these changes. Consumers want to recover an active role in the definition of the products they need. Pollution levels are forcing us to find new solutions to reduce the environmental impact of industrial development. Workplaces must become more pleasant to attract the younger generations who, for the first time in history, have averagely risen above the first steps of the Maslow scale and are looking for further gratifications and personal satisfaction. Studies, research and experiments are being carried out all over the world to identify the outlines of the post-industrial company.

The Post-industrial Company

The premiss is that future economic and productive systems will have to base themselves on greater creative capabilities (given the rising difficulties in standardizing) and on flexibility. Flexibility is perhaps the keyword of the new system, and the word is taken in its widest sense. If it is flexible a company can tackle the continuous changes in the needs of customers, the environment, technology and business strategies. To satisfy these requisites it will be necessary to:

• Separate organizations into small operative units
• Use horizontal information networks, not hierarchical ones
• Use actively the brains of everyone in all operative positions

Company organization will therefore change profoundly. The same group of people will have to be able to produce both the hardware and the software of a product. Today software is produced in offices, the hardware in factories. People will work together on problems and new opportunities, even over long distances, using information networks, creating ad hoc groups for all types of necessity. Even companies will be able to combine together in various ways according to necessity. Thus a company may be both supplier and customer of another company at one and the same time, competitor or ally, according to the object of the moment – is business.

The small scale will be normal and it will be made possible by microelectronics, close interaction and mutual dependence between producers and consumers, probably physically close at hand. Company organization will be based on numerous inter-active nuclei made up into groups and sub-groups able to respond creatively to the continuous changes of scenario and market – this will be considered routine. This type of company and factory is defined as holonic units. The system created by connecting up such companies and units through information networks and shared management systems is called a holonic system.

An idea of the virtual-holonic enterprise. What is a virtual-holonic enterprise? It is defined thus: a group of autonomous operative units that act together in an integrated, organic manner within a holonic network system, configuring itself each time it is neces-sary as a value chain most adapted to pursue the business opportunities the market offers. The autonomous operative units mentioned here can be small companies or parts of compa-nies. This definition makes it clear that we are talking about a highly developed organization that goes beyond what has been invented by collective creativity so far.

It may also be helpful to define what is "not" a holonic system:

- A group of individual companies that interact with market logics in a regime of free competition and alliances – this is the present situation that enables us to have only a partial vision and causes unnecessary efforts to be wasted on local conflicts
- An alliance of companies acting in the same sector – this would simply be good for lobbying; such companies would be excluded from the real business chains that cross the sector

- A purely information network – apart from the costs necessary, this would not give any added value other than the speed of communications
- A series of companies open to each other – this would simply help to develop better benchmarking and Comakership processes
- A series of long-term contracts between customers and suppliers – this would simply set up Comakership situations which would be conditioned in the long run by those operating on the final market
- A consortium of companies – this would limit itself to cost reduction objectives or the creation of scale economies or marketing activities without changing the structure of the company
- A partnership and/or a joint venture – this would include only two or a few more companies at a time, all very specific

While it is true that the combination of some of these factors can be useful to the development of a planned strategy, the virtual-holonic enterprise requires something more: the activation of a system of autonomous operative units, distributed over the territory, covering different roles, with the common mission of pursuing common business ends. To give an idea of the rationale with which a virtual-holonic enterprise should operate, I will cite a recent example that will help to explain the functional rationale of an integrated business chain, although it still cannot be defined a complete virtual-holonic enterprise.

An American business chain in the textile and clothing sector substantially modified its way of doing business. All the potential players in the business took part simultaneously in the designing process of the new operational method: yarn makers, weavers, garment manufacturers and distributors (department stores/sales outlets). The driving force behind the study was a crisis in the sector – stress situations help a great deal toward the search for daring solutions!

The main factor in the crisis had been identified as the problem of costs (they were uncompetitive compared with Far Eastern countries). However there existed a possible lever of competitive advantage in the times involved in their supply chain (time passing between spinning the yarn and the final sales outlet of the made-up garment). It was potentially determined by the long transport times (and relative costs) burdening the Far Eastern production. Until then the US industry had not managed to exploit this advantage. Despite the long distances the Far Eastern competitors did not reveal such a large gap (indeed their supply chain was so fluid upstream that it often managed to compensate abundantly for the problem of greater transport times). A work group was created with the general managers/entrepreneurs of the chain who could be potentially interested. An analytical approach was applied (in this case Theory of Constraints) to see how the total costs of the whole chain might be reduced while at the same time gaining a competitive advantage in terms of response times. The objectives were reached by adopting the following solution: each company participating in the chain would be paid only when the final customer bought the finished product. This new rule has made all the companies involved competitive again. In fact the chain managed to activate at great speed and autonomously both Time Based Organization and Total Quality Management, with all the competitive advantages these strategies can create.

In the new context each company:

• Avoided surplus production, being concerned to manufacture as late as possible and only what would effectively be sold (because it would be paid only for what would actually be sold at the sales point)
• Avoided manufacturing beforehand, so as not to create stocks, indeed attempting to wait as long as possible to have more reliable sales forecasts (in practice applying just in time)
• Tried to produce very small batches, with a continuous supply flow, to avoid the risk of unsold goods and limit process stocks (in practice applying Lean Production)
• Insisted on being connected in real time with the information system of the sales outlets and the whole business chain, so as to be able to react precisely, with direct data not mediated or altered in times and quantities (for example, the direct data generated by bar code scanning on the products sold and registered at the cash desks)

The result was that the total costs of the whole chain were reduced so significantly (specially in stocks and returns) that it could almost compete with the total costs of the Far Eastern supplies (burdened by a higher materials outstanding). More than this, however, what made the US solution a winner were the times. The supply and reaction times of the chain were reduced to such a point that they could exploit all the sales peaks in real time, without reserve stocks, to the utmost satisfaction of the sales outlets who could thus sell more than planned of the most popular articles.

No delay in the cash flow occurred because the suppliers had been paid some time after delivery in the preceding system anyway and stockage costs of all the companies involved were reduced with the new system. The financial cost of the operation was therefore insignificant, or even negative. This example gives an idea of the unconventional solutions that can be generated by an approach based on the perfecting of value chains rather than any partial approach, based on the perfecting of individual companies.

I will now attempt a generalization that can cover various possible combinations and also introduce some more advanced concepts of the example cited. The basic requisites for the creation of a virtual enterprise can be expressed with the following guidelines:

- All the components of the virtual enterprise must have and share a vision of what they want to achieve
- Shared (although dynamic) rules must be established
- A network of companies throughout the territory must be set up with adequate connections between them
- There must be a common information system operating in real time
- A flexible, interactive, open staff system must be set up
- Highly flexible and agile production and management systems must be set up
- Channels must be activated for pro-sumers, which enable the competitive advantage to be transformed into real product value

The "hard" or physical parts and the micromanagement parts required by this model are almost entirely achievable with the innovative approaches and ingredients already introduced to European companies in recent years (Total Quality, Lean Organization, BPR, Simultaneous Engineering). The macrostructural and infrastructural parts need to be examined further. In the first place it is obvious that a system so definitely oriented towards business and the market can only be market driven. Therefore no theoretical, aesthetical or symmetrical consideration can hold good. The virtual enterprise must be structured as a function of the fundamental processes or of competitive advantage linked to the various companies, seen from the point of view of the final customer. There can therefore be:

- Technological virtual enterprises, where the principal business factor, and at the same time the value of the output is prevalently determined by technological capabilities and know-how (the US's Silicon Valley, Italy's Prato a few years ago)
- Business chain virtual enterprises (such as the garment example already illustrated)
- Virtual enterprises centred on integrator roles (for instance, for computers or for technologies where important soft and hard components must be combined, and also for customized engineering processes, and so on)

It is worth mentioning that virtual-holonic enterprises which are by constitution dynamic, with a variable configuration in time, can include configurations already set up for a fixed term (for example, for important plant engineering projects). Business areas and sectors with semi-permanent configurations like the car manufacturing sector, informatics, consumer electronics are probably the most frequent type. These developments confirm the industrial systems' increasing trend towards greater outsourcing (the decentralization of processes and activities not considered core technologies). Take the example of Europe's car manufacturing industry. To keep in line with the Japanese and US producers they expect to increase decentralization of their activities to 30% in the next few years.

These first indications on this type of enterprise provide useful hints on the construction of an organizational model particularly adapted to tackling more complex competitive scenarios. However, the general characteristics of virtual-holonic enterprises and their differences from other organizational forms must make us think more deeply about their functional and operative requisites. The two most fundamental prerequisites are:

1 The existence of a holonic network system
2 The capacity to operate as a virtual enterprise

The first of these reduces to a minimum both transactional costs and decision-making time, which are the limiting barriers of present network systems. It provides the infrastructure system that makes it possible to develop the economic subject producing value for the market (the virtual enterprise itself). The second prerequisite provides market-driven organizations oriented to real added value. Let us now see how these prerequisites become operational methods.

The operative structure of virtual-holonic enterprises. The creation and development of a virtual-holonic enterprise are possible only if there exists a holonic system that makes available the necessary technical and organizational capabilities. These will be used by the virtual enterprises selectively and precisely. There are three basic types of autonomous operational unit in a virtual-holonic enterprise:

1 The resource units
2 The operational units
3 The integrating units

They are activated in real time thanks to the holonic network mechanisms but they can be started up at different points of time. Operative units carrying out very different types of activity can be found in each category. The common denominator is the type of function and the role they have in the holonic system.

The resource units are there to provide the other operative units with the core business factors (the factors which form the nucleus of the generated value). These factors, either singly or combined in different ways, can be identified as follows:

- Development and supervision of product and/or service know-how
- Development of the persons capable of producing the business performance
- Development and supervision of any necessary specializations
- Market strategies
- Financing

More generally the resource units supervise the core components of the whole business chain and find the assets necessary to create it.

The operational units manage the business operatively. They can be distributed along the whole business chain in cascade (one produces, the other commercializes) or they can be verticalized in parallel (producing and commercializing different product lines in parallel). They depend on the resource units for technology exchanges, training, communication networks or specialized consultancy. A good operative unit can carry out many of these functions on its own. The principle is to keep them lean and to outsource the supply of resources. Operational units also develop technology (both productive and for distribution) so as to constantly improve competitivity in terms of costs, quality, flexibility, reliability and response times. Competitive comparisons are made both with other units in the same system and with units belonging to other holonic systems.

The integrating units combine the outputs of various resource units and operational units. For example they may connect a unit with product know-how with a software producer and a hardware producer, and then supply the result to a sales unit and/or a technical assistance unit. An integrating unit must therefore constantly improve its capacity to know the outside world, both in the holonic system to which it belongs and in other holonic systems. Benchmarking becomes strategically important as it is one of the essential business instruments. It is the integrating units that generate most added value. However, the virtual-holonic system obliges them to distribute this added value equally among all the nodes in the system. Sharing transparent systems for measuring performance means respecting the rules of the system which have been accepted at the begin-

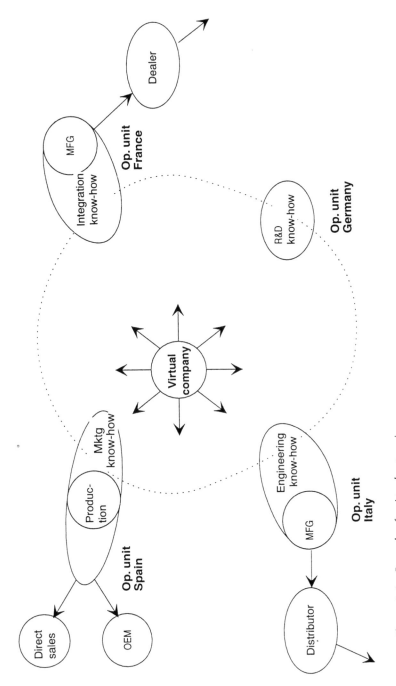

Figure 9.4 *Example of a virtual enterprise.*

the rules of the system which have been accepted at the beginning – and this is an essential condition for a holonic system.

Such an organization may sacrifice high economic returns in the short term to the advantage of a more stable global equilibrium over the longer term. In these conditions the other units could remove it from its place if they are not satisfied by its performance, and choose another unit. Business could thus carry on without being conditioned by any unsatisfactory units.

The differences with the roles existing in consortia of companies or in industrial areas should be observed. A graphic example of a virtual-holonic enterprise is shown in Figure 9.4.

Glossary

Acceptable quality level (AQL)   Highest percentage of defective elements (or highest number of defects per 100 units) to be considered satisfactory as an average performance of a process for acceptance sampling. It is identified with a particular plan and corresponds approximately to the quality associated with producer risk.

Action SEDAC   This is probably the most innovative and effective form of SEDAC. It is related in cascade with the Sub SEDAC (see below) and the Master SEDAC (see below) that generate it. This does not mean it is to be used universally. It is chosen when there is a need to improve the performance of existing activities by improving the operating methods already in use in the company. It is not suitable to develop innovative projects for which Project Groups are suggested. It is the organizational form that should be used most after Individual Tasks because it involves the most common type of improvement.

Activity Based Costing (ABC)   Approach to cost management based on a vision of business as a series of activities, each of which absorbs resources. It supersedes the old cost accounting concept that products absorb resources (and cost proportionately), substituting it with the new concept that the activities consume resources and the products consume activities. The cost of a product is therefore the result of the number of activities it consumes (e.g. production, moving, supplying, designing, research, etc.). ABC was developed to determine product cost. Its areas of application have lately been amplified to include other sectors such as management control, cost analysis along the life cycle of the product, market profitability analyses.

Activity Based Management (ABM) Management approach based on Management by Processes (see below) using ABC (see above) operatively.

Audit Official, systematic examination of all a company's functions, making use of adequate information sources. There are basically three types of audit: the system audit, the process audit and the product audit.

Autonomation Productive system in which the machinery or plant is designed to stop automatically and emit an alarm signal whenever waste or anomalies are registered. It is a component of the Jidohka system.

Benchmarking Structured, permanent approach which compares the products/processes of one's own company with those of the market leaders. These leaders may or may not belong to the same commodity sector. The gap separating one's company from the market leader are quantified and analyzed to define objectives and improvement plans.

Best Practices The best applications in the world from the point of view of specific performances or indicators.

B–Q Matrix Used in Management by Processes to evaluate company processes according to their importance for business and the quality of performances achieved (effectiveness and efficiency). Analysis of these parameters gives the four process types:
1 Processes to be redesigned
2 Processes for which a Breakthrough improvement is necessary
3 Processes for which Daily Routine Work (DRW) (see below) is necessary

4 Processes in which the present performances can be maintained

Breakthrough Drastic improvement of a given operating performance, making a clean break with preceding performances.

Budget Tool by which a company plan is drawn up and expressed. The budget-making process coordinates the activities of the different functions of a company. The budgetary system of a company is formed of more than one budget and includes the master budget, the sales budget, the production budget, the purchasing budget, the outlay budget and the investment budget. Once passed, budgets are a point of reference when controlling results.

Business plan Company plan indicating the objectives it is intended to pursue over the short and medium time span regarding strategy, turnover, costs and profits. It is usually accompanied by the budget (see above) and cash flow. It is usually prepared in monetary terms on the product-family level. The business plan, the sales plan and the operative plan are frequently prepared on different levels of detail but they must be elaborated coherently and maintained so.

Business processes Company processes with a conditioning impact on the business results. They can be primary processes (see below) or support processes (see below).

Business Process Reengineering (BPR) Thorough rethinking and radical redesigning of processes to obtain drastic improvements in their performances (costs, quality, service, speed).

Cash flow Amount of finances effectively produced by a company over a given period. It is found by calculating the difference between the cash takings and the cash outlays during the period considered.

CEDAC Diagram Component of the SEDAC system (see below). The cause-and-effect diagram with addition of cards is both a tool and an "organizational form" for the management of improvement projects. The diagram is physically represented by a board. It is put on view in the department where a problem is generated and monitored continuously. Everybody can contribute to finding the solution by attaching different coloured cards containing information on real obstacles or causes and their ideas for improvement. It is a highly effective support in the pursuit of continuous daily improvement because:

- It constantly attracts everybody's attention to an important problem the company wants to overcome
- It gathers and displays ideas coming from many people without the need to organize meetings
- It informs everybody in real time of the process being analyzed and of new standards thus providing "on-the-spot management"

Certification   Certification of the quality system of a production or service company means the formal act of recognition that the company has carried out a series of planned and documented activities to make its products/services comply with certain standards. Certification must be by a nationally or internationally recognized organization. The International Standards Organization 9000 series of regulations is usually taken as the reference model for the development and certification of the quality system. These regulations are also the basis of the Italian system of standardization, UNI, with the UNI-EN 29000 regulations.

Check points   This term is used to define all the data on a specific performance (control cards, compliance percentages, etc.), gathered daily to monitor a process. Check point data are summarized by the indicators relative to the Control Points (see below).

Codesign   Cooperation on the design stage of a new product between customer and supplier. The supplier is asked to develop a product or component, quite autonomously and with full responsibility, on the basis of the customer's functional specifications. This must be done respecting the general objectives established (e.g. quality, times, costs) to satisfy the final customer. Codesign is a qualifying element of Comakership (see below) and is executed by extending the organizational/methodological approaches of Simultaneous Engineering (see below) to the suppliers.

Comakership Purchasing strategy where suppliers are closely involved in improvement activities so as to obtain competitive advantages in quality, service, innovation and cost. It is based on authentic collaboration between customer and suppliers and on the sharing of the competitive advantage. It requires consolidated relations with the suppliers, an evaluation and global qualification of the suppliers and interactive customer–supplier collaboration

Computer Aided Design (CAD) The use of information systems by designers when preparing a product. It may include the following functions:
- Coding and classifying the parts
- Designing
- Modelling
- Project analysis
- Defining the technical specifications
- Documentation management
- Design data-base management
- Interfaces

Computer Aided Engineering (CAE) The use of computer systems to develop the calculations necessary to simulate the real production conditions of a designed product. By creating a model based on the design, simulations can be made of functional, structural and performance aspects of a product.

Computer Integrated Manufacturing (CIM) With this philosophy technology and information systems are introduced into a company while maintaining a coherent global vision. The production process is integrated by an architecture connecting all the automation levels of the company. The information system is extended to designing and the organization of product development and to administrative activities.

Control points   Term used to define synthetic performance indicators (e.g. punctual delivery, PPM, etc.) based on specific data (check points, see above) recorded and gathered at the operating level. Control points are particularly used in Management by Policy (see below).

Core business processes   See primary processes.

Cost of Quality   The cost of not doing things right the first time.

Critical processes   Processes which are operating in an unsatisfactory way, having a negative impact on company business performance.

Customer satisfaction strategy   One of the basic strategies of Total Quality according to which the customer is the company's absolute priority. In practice this strategy unites a series of related priority decisions. A new managerial system emerges from these decisions, making a revolutionary break with the past. The decisions are made in reference to Quality, meaning the quality of everything expressed by the company.

Customer Survey   The objective of such surveys is to identify the aspects/elements of a product/service which are considered most important by customers and the degree of customer satisfaction (also compared with the competition). Such surveys enable a company to apply a market-in (see below) approach when evaluating its organization and performances critically, as it helps identify internal problems regarding the "customer satisfaction" objective.

Daily Routine Work (DRW)   Basic important process in Total Quality. It maintains performance levels in every company process and an incremental performance improvement. It can be applied in each organizational unit of the company, even at an individual level. DRW is:
- A managerial process (what)
- Carried out by every company unit (who)
- Pursuance of the objective of full customer satisfaction (why)

- Systematic control and continuous improvement (how)
- Every activity/process to which it is applied (where)
- On a daily, permanent basis (when)

Day to Day Management (DDM)   Supervision and continuous management in all a company's activities/processes with the aim of satisfying internal clients. Substantially equivalent to DRW (see above).

Delayering   Series of organizing analysis methodologies and tools that redesign roles to define flat, flexible structures.

Design for Assembly and Design for Manufacturing   Procedures devoting extreme attention to the development of a new product and its manufacture, right from the first phases. The number of components and the cost of the product are reduced by simplification while maintaining high quality objectives.

Design of Experiment (DOE)   Procedures developed to improve the effectiveness and efficiency of experimentation. They are used to evaluate the influence of certain parameters and their relative interactions on the result, having established realistic a priori experimental values of the parameters.

Design Review (DR)   Critical re-examination of a design carried out on a systematic, planned and interfunctional basis to ensure that the designer has used all the knowledge, methods and norms available to satisfy customer needs and at the same time perfect the product's life-cycle costs.

Effective Management   Management system aimed at obtaining important operative results quickly (see Breakthrough), so as to guarantee success in both the short term and the medium to long term.

Employee Satisfaction Survey   The aim of these surveys is to evaluate the degree of employee satisfaction in an organization. It is measured by the ratio between employee expectancy (elements/factors considered most important and their priorities) and employees' perception of the reality of the facts (situation perceived according to the elements/factors).

European Foundation for Quality Management (EFQM) Founded in 1988 to carry out the following roles:
- To accelerate the acceptance of quality as a strategy for global competitive advantage
- To stimulate and assist the deployment of quality improvement activities

Failure Mode and Effects Analysis (FMEA) Qualitative analysis of every possible type of failure in a system, identification of the resulting effects on the system, the functionality, and the personnel using it and the causes generating it. The outputs are preventive countermeasures modifying the project or controls in the company processes. The technique is used particularly in the designing stage to identify potential failure modes in a system/device and the most suitable corrective actions. It is applied to both product and process design.

Failure Mode and Effects Improvement (FMEI) Refers to the combination of FMEA (see above) and SEDAC (see below) used to tackle problems of product or process reliability improvement.

Flat and flexible structures Companies with a limited number of hierarchical levels and barriers between functions. They can guarantee fast, effective responses to changes in the market and customers' needs.

Flowac Combination of SEDAC (see below) and a flow diagram. Its use is suggested when improvements are to be made on a process or a procedure.

Forward Engineering Global approach to the development, design and engineering of high quality products in the shortest possible time and at the lowest possible costs.
The "quality" objective is based on QFD (see below) and envisages two areas: the capacity to design products with elevated customer satisfaction potentials (compliance with purpose);

and the capacity to drastically reduce "non quality" costs due to modifications to the product or machinery, production problems, customers' problems when using the product (technical assistance).

The "time to market" objective (see below) is pursued by approaches that reduce total development times (see Simultaneous Engineering), particularly by reviewing the whole development process and reducing the times of each single stage.

The "cost" objective is pursued at the same time as the two preceding objectives by such approaches and techniques as DOE (see above), Design for Assembly (see above) and Design for Manufacturing (see above), VA (see below), reliability techniques and strategic approaches such as codesign (see above), carry over and the mushroom concept (see below).

Gross operating margin May be defined as the difference between proceeds and cash costs related to the purchase–transformation–sale sequence. It is used to reintegrate the capital consumed in production, to remunerate the financial capital and to pay taxes.

Group Technology (GT) Production organization based on production units which manufacture a given family of parts in flow. In CAD/CAM (see above) it is a classification and coding system aiding the search for parts with similar shapes. The GT approach is useful in the passage from job shop to flow shop organization.

Individual task Organizational form in which the responsibility for a project target or for specific action is assigned to a single individual. It is statistically the most widely-used organizational form and is advised when specific actions or projects must be carried out which have a high specialization/technical content that can only be managed by one person. Otherwise they are advised for relatively simple actions/objectives.

Just in time (JIT) Organizational and management approach which includes:
• A production organization emphasizing the importance of operative flows and not productive-phase efficiency

- Continuous efforts to eliminate waste and improve quality by making problems visible (by reducing stocks) and attacking the causes
- the use of all the knowledge and experience available in the company, at all levels, including that of the operative personnel

JIT enables a company to produce the necessary products, of the necessary quality, in the quantity necessary, at the necessary moment and lowest cost.

Kaizen   Improvement obtained by involving the personnel, made by small steps, and operating on the existing situation. It requires much commitment by the personnel and limited investments.

Lead Time   The time that passes between the beginning of the first and the end of the last of a series of activities. In a productive-logistics field it is the period of time that goes from the birth of a need (an order, a requirement, etc.) and the availability of what is requested (delivery). The Lead Time is equal to the sum of the times necessary to carry out all the sequential activities, including the operative activities, set-ups, controls, pauses and transportation.

Lean organization   Organizational method with three reference criteria:
1   A flattening of the structure (reduction of the number of hierarchical levels/vertical divisions)
2   A shortening of the structure (reduction of the horizontal division)
3   Amplification of roles (widening of control breadth)

Lean Production   Production system introduced at Toyota by Eiji Toyoda and Tajichi Ohno. It typically uses a minimum level of company resources (personnel, space, plant, time, stocks) and is characterized by high quality products and the capacity to produce a wide variety of products. Lean Production unites the advantages of craft production with those of mass production. Multi-specialized teams of personnel at all levels are used, together with highly automated, flexible plant. It transfers the highest possible number of responsibilities to those workers who effectively create the added value of the product in production. It also forms a defect identifying system that finds the real origins of problems.

Learning organization   Organization able to learn and make improvements by combining continuous improvement capabilities with micro-innovation.

Management by Policy (MBP)   Fundamentally important managerial dimension of Total Quality. It is an annually-based management process applying company strategy at the operational level, transforming strategic objectives into results. As such Management by Policy is a process with which:
- Annual operative policies are defined on the basis of the medium- and long-term ones
- These policies are brought into practice by a process with concrete actions, in which the whole of the company structure participates

From another point of view MBP may be considered a series of activities with which a company makes important improvements in well-defined areas annually.

Management by Processes   As in MBP (where one to three priority objectives are identified, see above), Management by Processes requires a small number of priority processes to be identified (between four and six), which have priority impact on the year's business activities or for the future.

Market-in   Company orientation to the market and customers' requirements in opposition to an orientation focused prevalently on internal problems.

Master SEDAC   Graphic base for the management of the objectives in a first-level X Matrix (see below). It contains a summary of the objectives of an operative unit leader or a Breakthrough objective. It is set up starting with the indicators and targets of the first level X Matrix. The Master SEDAC objective is to supply all the elements necessary for the visual control system of the indicators of a performance to be improved and all the improvement activities to achieve the planned objectives.

Mushroom concept   Product structure which proceeds almost unvaried in the first part of the graph and then explodes at the last stages of the transformation process. The structure both of the product and of the processes (technological layout) therefore makes a mushroom-like shape. The result is to obtain more flexible products, more easily personalized and at lower costs, having reduced the number of codes managed.

On Error Training   This is the use of errors as the basis of analyses aimed at improving later performances. It is used regularly to eliminate waste.

Overall Equipment Effectiveness (OEE)   This is the total efficiency of a plant/machine. It is expressed in percentages and relates the real operating time to the machine loading time. The operating time is found by subtracting from the machine loading time, the times of the six big losses:

1   Breakdowns and unexpected events
2   Set-up (see below) and adjustments
3   No-load running times and brief stoppages
4   Reductions of speed
5   Rejects (see below) during the process
6   Start-up rejects

PDCA (Plan, Do, Check, Act)   Developed by Deming, the "PDCA cycle" is the basic construction block with which to pursue effectiveness in improving and maintaining processes and company performances. PDCA is effected by a cyclical action with four basic stages:

1   Plan: prepare a plan thoroughly.
2   Do: carry out what has been decided in the plan stage.
3   Check: check the results and compare them with what has been planned.
4   Act: decide whether to maintain the plan as it is or adjust it.

Each of these stages is made up of a PDCA sub-cycle. In practice the application of PDCA combines numerous mental approaches behind Total Quality:

- Analyzing the data and talking with the facts in hand
- Concentrating on a few basic priorities
- Looking for the causes and the causes of the causes
- Checking further and further back
- Applying statistical analysis to all problems
- Tending towards prevention, not cure
- Giving emphasis to preparation/approach, not to remedying
- Focusing on the process rather than its output

Performance drivers Basic factors influencing the performances of an activity. They are used in ABM systems (see above).

PERTAC This is a combination of SEDAC (see below) and the PERT Diagram (see below). It is found most useful in fields where the business is customized (engineering or production), where it is advisable to concentrate on the critical paths.

Policy Deployment One of the basic methods in Total Quality because it enables Management by Policy to be carried out and also because it is an indispensable technique to prepare any improvement activity. Policy Deployment is defined as being the organizational and methodological process by which an objective or policy can be rationally divided up into:

- Areas of intervention
- Sub-objectives
- Methods (types of action)
- Responsibilities and resources necessary

As an organizational process Policy Deployment is one of the six phases of Management by Policy. It is used to plan how to reach the most important objectives of the business plan.

Primary processes Also called core business processes. They are defined as being all the company processes which have a major impact on company business and are characteristic of the sector in which the company operates.

Priority processes   Processes that are important for the business performances and, at the same time, are today badly performed, thus representing business bottlenecks, the first processes to be improved in a Management by Process logic.

Process capability   Capacity of a process to satisfy specific requests in output. In practice it is the relationship between the curve showing the dispersion degree of process performances and the specific requests. In a Gaussian distribution the process capability index is identified as the ratio between the upper and lower specific difference (tolerance) and the average quadratic deviation multiplied by six.

Process control   The various activities through which the development of a given process takes place while obtaining the desired results and in compliance with its purpose.

Process Owners   Those responsible for the processes in Managing by Process.

Product carry over   Strategy influencing the development of new products. It is the decision to reduce changes in components influencing product image, carrying over components that have proved themselves reliable, to be sure there will be fewer risks of defects (greater reliability) and lower costs. This approach is usually used together with a reduction in product life cycle.

Programme Evaluation and Review Technique (PERT) Scheduling technique that identifies the links existing between the various activities necessary to complete a given project. It identifies the activities themselves (shown by an arrow) and the events with which each activity begins or ends (shown by a circle). Once all the activities and their relative times have been prepared the PERT enables the critical path to be identified, the sequence of activities and events that require the most time.

Project Group   Three to seven people (typically middle managers) from various functions, chosen to tackle an improvement project. They use PDCA (see above) problem-finding and problem-solving methods. They generally meet on a regular basis (a meeting once every week or two weeks) and are guided by a leader who is either already nominated or is elected by them. The group breaks up at the end of the project (which should not last more than four to six months if it is to maintain effectiveness). Project Groups should only be used when innovative or complex projects need to be developed, given the commitment in time and organization they require.

Project management All the methods and techniques, both managerial and organizational, used to plan and control projects. Together they are applied in the overall management of large projects, in the management of production orders in companies working on customized products, and in the management of non-recurring activities within a specific project in companies not normally working on customized products, e.g. the development of a new project, the study and construction of a new plant, etc.

Pull system System in which production is activated in response to utilization or to replace what has been utilized. Release dates and ultimation dates are assigned to the last stage of the process. The various stages of the process are scheduled backwards with the ultimation dates being defined within each stage.

Quality Assurance This is normally defined as being the series of activities, programmes and planned systematic actions necessary to provide adequate assurance that a product or service satisfies established quality requisites.

Quality Control in management "Quality Control" here means the Quality Control techniques which are based on the Quality Control Concept. Application of this concept concerns three main areas:
1 *Activities directly related to the product/service.* This means marketing, product development etc., right through to post-sales assistance. It is by this total application that it can be seen how Total Quality provides Quality Assurance of products/services;

2 *Activities not directly related to the product/service.* Quality Control must also be applied to the various activities not directly related to the product/service (budget, investment plan, technology development plan);

3 *Company management.* It is in this field that the Quality Control concept becomes a full managerial tool. It provides the approach and the methodology at all levels of the company management process, starting from the chairperson.

Quality Function Deployment (QFD)   Development/planning technique of a product/service which enables one:

- To identify the expectations and needs of the client and to transform and transfer them correctly into product and process specifications
- To reduce the need for corrections and later modifications to the product and in the technological processes
- To reduce the costs and development times

Quantum leaps   Numerous, continuous quantitatively important leaps forward in company performances.

Return on assets (ROA)   Company productivity index relating current profits in percentage (with the addition of the net financial burden) to the net assets.

Robust Design (RD)   Design approach aimed at determining the most stable and therefore most robust configuration of a system. A system is considered robust when, besides satisfying the requirements for which it was designed, it does not amplify the imperfections inherent in the design and construction processes but attenuates them on a performance response level.

SEDAC Diagram   Diagrams drawn on boards which are put up in the departments or offices where there is a problem to eliminate or a performance to improve. The main types of SEDAC diagram are the CEDAC (see above), the PERTAC (see above), the FLOWAC (see above) and the FMEI (see above).

SEDAC system   The Sedac system was devised by the Deming prizewinner Ryuji Fukuda. The name is an acronym standing for Structure for Enhancing Daily Activities through Creativity. Its scope is to improve daily activities by stimulating creativity. The operative system is based on the use of post-it type cards. The operative instruments, Action SEDACs (see above) are made up of various types of SEDAC Diagrams (see above).

Self-certification   A customer considers a supplier to be self-certified when his quality management system and products are found to respond so well to the customer's requirements that it is unnecessary to make any kind of routine or acceptance control.

Set-up   The time necessary to organize the passage from one product to the next in a given workplace. It is equal to the time that passes between the production of the last valid piece (i.e. free from defects and produced in normal running conditions) of one product and the first of the new product. In time order it is divided up into:
1   Internal set-up: elements of the set-up procedure carried out while the machine is idle.
2   External set-up: elements of the set-up procedure carried out while the machine is running.

Seven management tools   These new instruments mainly employ qualitative/verbal data rather than the quantitative/numerical data of the seven statistical tools (see below). Their purpose is to aid problem-finding activities by organizing and analyzing the elements. They are:
1   Affinity Diagram
2   Connections Diagram
3   Tree Diagram (see below)
4   Matrix Diagram
5   Decision Tree
6   PERT Arrow Diagram (see above)
7   Data-Matrix Analyses

Seven statistical tools   Technical approach belonging to Total Quality. These instruments are the result of the adaptation to industry of scientific methods. With these tools anybody can acquire a scientific approach and many problems can be solved. They are:

1   Data gathering
2   Stratification
3   Pareto diagram
4   Cause-and-effect diagram
5   Correlation diagram
6   Histogram
7   Control card

Shelf Engineering System with which new products are designed using a large proportion of ready-made modules kept ready on the (electronic) shelf. It is helpful in developing product carry-over technologies (see above).

Simultaneous Engineering Organizing approach similar to Forward Engineering and Concurrent Engineering, the purpose of which is to reduce the completion times of the new product development. It reduces the need to work on site and brings forward phases that otherwise are carried out later, placing them in parallel with the preceding phases and eliminating the transfers of the assignment between the groups involved in development which are typical of traditional approaches.

Special management A management process which focuses on one to three numerical objectives for which important objectives have been planned. The operative plan for the special management of priorities makes it possible:
- To have a specific programme of responsibilities and actions focused on the priority objectives (not on the meandering details of budget data)
- To identify the indicators to manage operatively (not merely the accounting data to balance)
- To assign ambitious and challenging objectives, shaking off the dangerous "objective = budget performance" mental set
- To involve the line directly in the planning, management and control of the company's priority objectives

Statistical Process Control (SPC) The use of statistics for an "economic" Process Control (see above). The statistical approach uses the concept of Inference to evaluate a series of events (products, data, information) by observing a small part of them (sample).

Study Group   These are made up of high level managerial staff, or of particularly competent staff members. The groups are almost always interfunctional and are set up when it is not clear how an objective must be tackled and an investigation is needed to make a decision. They are first-phase forms of organization which generate organizational forms suitable to the approach chosen. They should not last more than a month.

Sub SEDAC   As with the Master SEDAC (see above), the Sub SEDAC is activated as a function of each second level and third level X Matrix.

Supply chain   Includes all the suppliers of raw materials and semi-manufactured materials, the manufacturers and assemblers of finished products and the distribution channels that contribute to creating the value and costs of a given product/service.

Support processes   Company processes that do not satisfy the conditions defining the primary processes (see above).

Theory of Constraints   Innovative problem-finding approach developed by Eliyahu M. Goldratt, based on the observation that the results of any organization are conditioned by the weakest link in its chain of activities. The theory presents an organized method for identifying the weak links, determining the best way to tackle them and focus improvement efforts on them. It is therefore an effective tool for identifying short- and medium-term priority objectives, especially when they are to be found in organization and management rather than in numerical facts.

Time to market   The time that passes between the beginning of the development process of a new product and the moment when it reaches the market. Being able to do this in a shorter time than the competition means having an important competitive advantage.

Total Industrial Engineering (TIE)   Integrated approach to production problems pursuing continuous improvement of methods and production organization by involving all the personnel and by the use of specific procedures. Its peculiar characteristics are:

- Emphasis on the efficiency of the whole system rather than the single departments
- Involvement of all the personnel, not only the specialists, in studying and carrying out improvement actions both in the organization and in production methods

Total Logistic Strategy (TLS)   Integrated, innovative management along the supply chain of the flow and warehousing of materials, parts and finished products, starting from the suppliers, through the company, down to the customer.

Total Manufacturing Management (TMM)   Model of production organization and operative management employing maximum involvement of human resources and the delegation of entrepreneurial tasks down through the company structure. It pursues one of the Total Quality objectives, which is to create a highly flexible production system with zero defects and minimum Lead Time (see above). Some of the most important criteria of TMM are:
- Organization by flows
- Fast set-ups
- Small batches
- High process reliability
- Great flexibility
- High product quality

Total Productive Maintenance (TPM)   Maintenance approach whose aim is to raise the global efficiency of plant by eliminating the six main causes of plant inefficiency (the six big losses). The approach means involving all the plant operators and forming small interfunctional groups centred on maintenance activities. A focal point of the TPM approach is the change in mentality required of the operators, who should tend to consider themselves as the owners of the plant rather than simple custodians.

Total Quality (TQ)   Wide range of Quality Control activities applied to all aspects of company operations. Professor Asak has defined TQ as "the systematic application of common sense". The objective of TQ is to attain the company's targets by designing, producing and distributing products and services in such a way as to obtain the clients' full satisfaction on the economic level.

Toyota production system   System based on the complete elimination of waste. This means the elimination of defective material and stocks in just in time production, producing the objects that are needed, when they are needed and in the quantity needed.

Tree Diagram   Aggregation/disaggregation method analyzing the numerous elements concurring to determine an observed phenomenon (anomaly, technical solution, design, information, etc.). It may be applied in fields such as:
- Analyses of the causal chains concurring to determine an anomaly
- Definition of the components, the stages of the activities necessary in a Work Breakdown Structure (WBS) project
- Definition of the basic specification of a complex product
- Identification of actions ensuring and improving quality
- Representation and structuring of company policies
- Detailed development of the activities of a company function
- Functional analysis of products in value analysis

Tree Diagrams are one of the seven management tools (see above).

Value Analysis (VA)   The aim of this tool is to improve product functionality and at the same time reduce costs. It is an analysis of each product and process of a company to see if the costs are reasonable compared with the price of the product or the value generated. The actions to be carried out on the methods and technologies to reduce their cost are then identified. VA is particularly important when it is applied to purchased materials.

Value chain   Tool for measuring the competitive position of a company, created by M.E. Porter. A company is broken up into its strategically relevant activities in order to reveal cost trends, and the existing and potential sources of differentiation. The company gains competitive advantage by its capacity to carry out these activities more economically and/or effectively than its competitors.

Vendor Rating   Global evaluation of supplier performance to check that the results can satisfy the prescriptions/exigencies of the customer. The analysis is exclusively based on objective, complete data which must summarize the supplier's actual conduct.

Virtual-holonic company   A group of autonomation companies that, acting in an integrated and organic manner, is able to configure itself to manage each business opportunity that a customer presents.

Vision   The image of the future the company intends to create for itself. Vision generates the creative tension necessary for the generative learning condition characteristic of learning organizations (see above). Creative tension stems from the contrast between what it wants to create and current reality.

Visual Control System (VCS)   This is used to supply all the people concerned in operative management with information in a clear and visible manner. The information may concern procedures, process/product indicators, advice, notices, etc.

Window Analysis   One of the components of the SEDAC system (see above). It is a technique that enables the nature of a problem to be coded and the actions to eliminate it to be identified. It is applied with a double entry matrix on which two groups or people involved in the problem compare their views on the cause behind the waste/problem. With Window Analysis problems can be classified into four categories:

1   Category A: the ideal condition
2   Category B: problems due to human error, "intentional" negligence, lack of time, distractions
3   Category C: problems related to lack of information/communications
4   Category D: problems related to the lack of the correct method of "recurrent prevention" of the problem

X Matrix   Tool creating an effective link between planning and operating management by mapping the organization necessary to achieve objectives. It contains the following information:

- The synthesis of the methods by which the objective is to be pursued and in particular of the chosen operating indicators
- The assignment of the target responsibilities on the indicators
- The reference policies associated with the various projects/actions
- The organizational forms set up to pursue such targets
- The timetable for the projects/actions

Zero Base Budget (ZBB) Short-term planning method for company activity. It is different from the classical budget (see above) because instead of taking as a reference the existing level of activity and outlay and noting rises and falls compared to this base, the Zero Base Budget reconsiders the entire company activity as though it were a new project.

Bibliography

ABEGGLEN J.C. and G. STALK jr., *Kaisha. The Japanese Corporation*, Basic Books, New York 1985.

AKAO Y., *Hoshin Kanri*, Productivity Press, Cambridge 1991.

AMES, *Market Driven Management*, Dow Jones Irwin, Homewood 1988.

BLACKBURN J.D., *Time Based Competition*, Business One Irwin, Homewood 1991.

COLLINS B. and E. HUGE, *Management by Policy*, Quality Press, Milwaukee 1993.

DAVIDOW H. and M. MALONE, *The Virtual Corporation*, Harper Collins, New York 1992.

FLORIDA R. and M. KENNEY, *The Breakthrough Illusion*, Basic Books, New York 1990.

GALGANO A., *Company Wide Quality Control*, Productivity, Portland 1994.

GOLDRATT E. and J. COX, *The Goal*, North River Press, New York 1994.

GRENIER R. and G. METES, *Going Virtual*, Prentice Hall, Englewood Cliffs, NJ 1995.

HAMMER M. and J. CHAMPY, *Reengineering the Corporation*, Harper Collins Publishers, New York 1994.

HARRINGTON H.J., *The Improvement Process*, McGraw-Hill, New York 1986.

HARTLEY J., *Concurrent Engineering*, Productivity Press, Cambridge 1992.

JOHANSSON H., P. McHUGH, A.J. PENDLEBURY and W.A. WHEELER III, *Business Process Reengineering*, John Wiley & Sons, Chichester 1993.

McHUGH P., G. MERLI and W.A. WHEELER III, *Beyond Business Process Reengineering*, John Wiley & Sons, Chichester 1993.

MASKELL B., *Performance Measurement for World Class Manufacturing*, Productivity Press, Cambridge 1991.

MERLI G., *Total Manufacturing Management. Production Organization for the 1990s*, Productivity Press, Cambridge 1990.

MERLI G., *Comakership (The New Strategies in Purchasing)*, Productivity Press, Cambridge 1991.

MERLI G., *Total Quality Management*, ISEDI, Turin 1991.

MERLI G., *Eurochallenge*, IFS, Bedford 1992.

MERLI G., *Breakthrough Management*, John Wiley & Sons, Chichester 1995.

MERLI G. and M. BIROLI, *Organizzazione e gestione per processi*, ISEDI, Turin 1995.

MONDEN Y., *Cost Management in the New Manufacturing Age*, Productivity Press, Cambridge 1992.

OBOLENSKY N., *Practical Business Re-engineering*, Gulf Publishing Company, Houston 1994.

PETERS T., *Liberation Management*, Macmillan, London 1992.

SACCANI G. and G. MERLI, *L'azienda olonico-virtuale*, Il Sole 24 Ore Libri, Milan 1994.

SANNO MANAGEMENT, DEVELOPMENT RESEARCH CENTER, *Vision Management Translating into Action*, Productivity Press, Cambridge 1992.

SEKINE K. and K. ARAI, *Kaizen for Quick Changeover*, Productivity Press, Cambridge 1992.

SENGE P.M., *The Fifth Discipline*, Doubleday Currency, New York 1990.

Index